30-Minute Diabetic Air Fryer

Cookbook for Beginners

Quick & Crispy Low-Carb, Low-Sugar Recipes for Balanced Blood Sugar, Perfect for Type 1, Type 2, and Pre-diabetes

Meghan Neal

Table of Contents

Introduction

Welcome to the 30-Minute Diabetic Air Fryer Cookbook for Beginners, where health, flavor, and convenience come together to make every meal a breeze! If you're looking for a way to enjoy delicious, diabetes-friendly dishes without spending hours in the kitchen, then this cookbook is your new go-to guide. Whether you're a busy professional, a parent juggling a full schedule, or just someone who loves simple, tasty recipes, this book is designed to make healthy cooking easy and enjoyable.

With diabetes, maintaining a balanced diet is key to keeping blood sugar levels in check, but that doesn't mean you have to sacrifice flavor or variety. The 30-Minute Diabetic Air Fryer Cookbook for Beginners is packed with over 100 mouthwatering recipes that prove eating healthy can be both satisfying and delicious. Using the magic of an air fryer, you'll be able to create meals that are crispy, flavorful, and made with less oil, making every dish a win for both your health and your taste buds.

This cookbook is perfect for anyone who is short on time but doesn't want to compromise on quality. Each recipe can be made in 30 minutes or less, meaning you'll spend less time cooking and more time enjoying your meals. With clear, step-by-step instructions, even beginners will feel confident and comfortable in the kitchen. If you're new to air frying or to cooking in general, you'll appreciate how accessible and easy-to-follow the recipes are.

Not sure where to start? No problem! This book includes a 28-day meal plan to take the guesswork out of meal planning. With a variety of dishes mapped out for you, from breakfasts and lunches to dinners, snacks, and desserts, you'll have everything you need to enjoy nutritious, well-rounded meals every day. Whether it's a quick Avocado Toast with Poached Egg for breakfast, a refreshing Shrimp Taco for lunch, or a hearty dinner like Lemon Garlic Chicken Thighs with Roasted Broccoli, this book offers something for every taste and occasion. Even better, you can still indulge in your favorite sweet treats with options like Brownie Bites and Pumpkin Spice Muffins—all designed to be diabetes-friendly without sacrificing flavor.

For those looking to keep track of their nutritional intake, each recipe includes a full nutritional breakdown, so you'll always know exactly what's in your meal. This makes it easy to stay on top of your health goals, whether you're monitoring carbs, sugar, or calories.

Additionally, you'll find plenty of air fryer tips and tricks to help you get the most out of this handy kitchen appliance. You'll learn how to achieve perfectly crispy results with less oil, ensuring that each meal is both tasty and healthy.

Whether you're a seasoned cook or a complete beginner, the 30-Minute Diabetic Air Fryer Cookbook for Beginners has something for everyone. With recipes that range from hearty meat dishes to plantbased options, you'll find plenty of variety to keep your meals exciting. Most importantly, every recipe is designed to be low-carb, low-sugar, and packed with flavor, proving that eating healthy doesn't have to be boring.

Ready to embark on your culinary journey? Grab your air fryer and dive into a world of quick, easy, and nutritious meals that support your health and keep your taste buds happy!

30-Minute Diabetic Air Fryer Cookbook for Beginners (Served for Two)

Welcome to Your Flavorful Air Fryer Adventure!

Congratulations! You've just taken the first step towards revolutionizing your kitchen and your health. Welcome to the "30-Minute Diabetic Air Fryer Cookbook for Beginners" – your passport to a world where delicious meets nutritious and where managing diabetes becomes a delightful culinary journey.

Imagine sinking your teeth into crispy, golden-brown delicacies that taste sinfully good but align perfectly with your health goals. That's the magic of air frying, and we're here to guide you every step of the way.

Why This Cookbook Will Change Your Life

1. **Diabetes-Friendly Feasts**: Every recipe is carefully crafted with your glucose levels in mind. Say goodbye to bland "diet" food and hello to meals that tantalize your taste buds while supporting your diabetes management.

2. **30-Minute Marvels**: In today's fast-paced world, who has hours to spend in the kitchen? Our recipes prove that you can whip up gourmet-quality, diabetes-friendly meals in just half an hour.

3. **Perfect Portions for Two**: Whether you're cooking for yourself and a partner or just want leftovers for tomorrow's lunch, our recipes are tailored to serve two. Its portion control made easy!

4. **Air Fryer Magic**: From crispy vegetables to juicy proteins and even guilt-free desserts, you'll discover how versatile your air fryer can be. It's not just about frying – it's about reimagining your favorite dishes in a healthier way.

5. **Beginner-Friendly**: New to air frying or diabetes management? Don't worry! We break everything down into easy-to-follow steps, complete with tips and tricks to make you feel like a pro in no time.

What Sets This Cookbook Apart

- **Comprehensive Nutritional Info**: Each recipe comes with detailed nutritional information, including carb counts, to help you make informed choices.
- **Flavor-First Philosophy**: We believe that healthy eating should never mean sacrificing taste. Get ready for an explosion of flavors in every bite!
- **Adaptive Cooking**: While our recipes are diabetes-friendly, they're designed to be enjoyed by everyone. We include tips for adapting dishes for various dietary needs.
- **Real Success Stories**: Throughout the book, you'll find inspiring stories from real people who have transformed their health with these recipes.
- **Full-Color Photos**: Every recipe is accompanied by a mouthwatering photo to inspire your culinary creativity.

Your Journey to Delicious Health Starts Here

This isn't just a cookbook; it's your comprehensive guide to enjoying life with diabetes. From understanding the science behind diabetes and nutrition to mastering the art of air frying, we've got you covered.

Get ready to:

- Master the basics of air frying and diabetes management
- Explore a world of flavors without worrying about your blood sugar
- Save time and energy in the kitchen
- Rediscover the joy of cooking and eating
- Take control of your health, one delicious meal at a time

So, are you ready to turn up the heat (or should we say the air?) and start your flavorful journey to better health? Let's dive in and discover how managing diabetes may be as simple as pushing a button on your air fryer!

Welcome to your new, delicious life. Your body and taste buds will appreciate it.

A Quick Primer on Low-Carb Eating

While not all recipes in this book are strictly low-carb, many embrace this principle to help manage blood sugar levels:

- **Focus on Protein and Healthy Fats**: These nutrients have minimal impact on blood sugar and help you feel satisfied.

- **Choose Complex Carbs**: When including carbohydrates, opt for whole grains, legumes, and vegetables rich in fiber.

- **Portion Control**: Even with low-carb recipes, portion size matters. Our recipes are portioned for two to help you manage your intake.

- **Balance is Key**: Remember, a healthy diabetic diet is about balance, not deprivation.

Low-Carb Swaps Chart (some examples)

High-Carb Food	Low-Carb Alternative
Rice	Cauliflower rice
Pasta	Zucchini noodles
Potato chips	Air-fried kale chips
Bread	Lettuce wraps
Mashed potatoes	Mashed cauliflower
Tortillas	Lettuce wraps or coconut flour tortillas
Pizza crust	Cauliflower crust or almond flour crust
French fries	Air-fried zucchini or turnip fries
Croutons	Roasted nuts or cheese crisps
Oatmeal	Chia seed or flaxseed porridge
Flour (for baking)	Almond flour or coconut flour
Milk	Almond milk or coconut milk (unsweetened)
Hash browns	Shredded zucchini or rutabaga hash browns

Air Fryer 101 - Your New Secret Weapon

Meet Your New Best Friend: The Air Fryer

Imagine a kitchen appliance that can fry, bake, roast, and grill – all while using minimal oil and maximizing flavor. That's the power of an air fryer, and it's about to become your new secret weapon in managing diabetes deliciously.

How Does It Work?

Consider an air fryer to be a tiny convection oven on steroids. Here's the magic behind it:

1. **Rapid Air Technology**: A heating element and a powerful fan work together to circulate hot air around your food at high speed.

2. **Maillard Reaction**: This is the same browning process that makes traditionally fried foods so irresistible. The air fryer achieves this with little to no oil!

3. **Even Cooking**: The circulating air ensures your food cooks thoroughly on both sides, removing the need for flipping in most cases.

Why It's a Game-Changer for Diabetics

1. **Drastically Reduced Oil**: Uses up to 75% less oil than traditional frying methods, helping with weight management and insulin sensitivity.

2. **Better Blood Sugar Control**: Lower fat content leads to more stable blood sugar levels.

3. **Nutrient Retention**: Quick cooking times help preserve heat-sensitive vitamins and minerals.

4. **Versatility**: From vegetables to lean proteins, you can cook a wide variety of diabetes-friendly foods quickly and easily.

Getting to Know Your Air Fryer

Every air fryer is a bit different, but most share these key components:

1. **Basket or Tray**: Where you place your food. It's usually removable for easy cleaning.

2. **Control Panel**: Depending on your model, you'll have buttons or a touch screen to set temperature, time, and cooking modes.

3. **Heating Element and Fan**: The dynamic duo that creates the air frying magic.

4. **Temperature Range**: Most air fryers operate between 200°F and 400°F.

5. **Timer**: Typically goes up to 30 minutes, perfect for our quick recipes!

Air Fryer Hacks for Diabetes-Friendly Cooking

1. **Preheat for Perfection**: Just 2-3 minutes of preheating can make a big difference in texture and cooking time.

2. **Embrace the Shake**: Halfway through cooking, give your basket a shake to ensure even crispiness.

3. **Spritz, Don't Drench**: A light spray of oil has a major role in getting that ideal golden-brown finish.

4. **Layer with Care**: Use air fryer racks to cook multiple items at once without overcrowding.

5. **Think Beyond Frying**: Your air fryer is great for roasting vegetables, cooking lean meats, and even baking diabetes-friendly desserts!

Cleaning and Maintenance

It's essential to keep your air fryer clean for both hygiene and optimal performance. Here's a quick guide:

1. **After Each Use**: Wash the removable parts with warm, soapy water. Most are dishwasher-safe!
2. **Deep Clean Monthly**: Use a soft brush to clean the heating element and fan area.
3. **Avoid Abrasive Cleaners**: They can damage the non-stick coating.
4. **Quick Tip**: Line the basket with parchment paper for easy cleanup (but don't block all the airflow!).

With these basics under your belt, you're ready to start your air-frying adventure. Prepare to have your taste buds amazed. Stabilize your blood sugar – all with the push of a button!

The Air Fryer Advantage: By the Numbers

Benefit	Traditional Frying	Air Frying
Oil Usage	Up to 3 cups	0-1 tablespoon
Calorie Reduction	-	Up to 70% fewer calories
Cooking Time	20-30 minutes	10-20 minutes
Nutrient Retention	Moderate	High
Ease of Cleanup	Challenging	Easy

Ready to get cooking? Let's move on to our first recipe and start your journey to delicious, diabetic-friendly meals!

Pancakes with Sugar-Free Berry Compote

Servings: 2 | **Prep Time:** 10 min | **Cook Time:** 15 min

Ingredients:

For the Pancakes:
- ½ cup almond flour
- 2 large eggs
- ¼ cup unsweetened almond milk
- ½ teaspoon baking powder
- ½ teaspoon vanilla extract
- ¼ teaspoon cinnamon
- 1 tablespoon melted butter or coconut oil
- Cooking spray or a little olive oil

For the Sugar-Free Berry Compote:
- ½ cup mixed berries (blueberries, raspberries, or strawberries)
- 1 tablespoon water
- ½ teaspoon lemon juice
- 1-2 drops liquid stevia or any preferred sugar-free sweetener

Instructions:

1. In a medium bowl, whisk together the almond flour, eggs, almond milk, baking powder, vanilla extract, cinnamon, and melted butter or coconut oil until smooth.
2. Spray silicone molds or small oven-safe dishes with cooking spray. Pour the pancake batter into the molds, filling each about halfway. Place the molds in the air fryer basket and cook at 350°F (175°C) for 10-12 minutes or until the pancakes are set and golden brown.
3. While the pancakes are cooking, combine the berries, water, and lemon juice in a small saucepan over medium heat. Cook for 5-7 minutes, stirring occasionally, until the berries break down into a sauce-like consistency. Add stevia to taste.
4. Remove the pancakes from the molds and top with the sugar-free berry compote. Serve warm.

Tips & Tricks:

- **Meal Prep:** The pancake batter can be made ahead and stored in the fridge for up to 24 hours. Reheat cooked pancakes in the air fryer or microwave.
- **Substitution Suggestions:** You can use coconut flour instead of almond flour, but reduce the amount to ¼ cup since it absorbs more liquid. For a dairy-free option, use coconut oil instead of butter.
- **Blood Sugar Management:** Almond flour is low in carbs and rich in fiber, making it an excellent choice for keeping blood sugar levels stable.

NUTRITION: Calories 220 | Carbs 8g | Protein 10g | Fat 17g | Fiber 4g | Sugar 3g

Avocado Toast with Poached Egg

Servings: 2 | **Prep Time:** 5 min | **Cook Time:** 10 min

Ingredients:
- 2 slices whole grain bread
- 1 ripe avocado, mashed
- 2 large eggs
- ½ teaspoon lemon juice
- Salt and pepper to taste
- Cooking spray or a little olive oil
- Optional toppings: red pepper flakes, chopped cilantro, cherry tomatoes, or microgreens

Instructions:

1. Toast the whole grain bread slices in the air fryer at 350°F (175°C) for 3-4 minutes or until crispy.
2. In a small bowl, mash the avocado with lemon juice, salt, and pepper. Set aside.
3. Spray small oven-safe ramekins with cooking spray. Crack one egg into each ramekin. Add 1 tablespoon of water to each. Place the ramekins in the air fryer basket and cook at 300°F (150°C) for 6-7 minutes, or until the egg whites are set and the yolks are still slightly runny.
4. Spread the mashed avocado evenly on the toasted bread slices. Gently remove the poached eggs from the ramekins and place one on each slice of toast.
5. Season with extra salt and pepper to taste. Add any optional toppings you like, such as red pepper flakes, chopped cilantro, or cherry tomatoes. Serve immediately.

Tips & Tricks:

- **Meal Prep:** You can prepare the avocado mash in advance, but keep it in an airtight container with the pit to prevent browning. Reheat the toast and eggs as needed.
- **Substitution Suggestions:** For a gluten-free option, use gluten-free bread. You can also add a sprinkle of feta cheese or swap lemon juice for lime for a different flavor.
- **Blood Sugar Management:** Whole grain bread provides fiber and slow-releasing carbs, helping to maintain stable blood sugar levels, while the healthy fats in avocado promote satiety.

NUTRITION: Calories 300 | Carbs 18g | Protein 11g | Fat 21g | Fiber 7g | Sugar 2g

Air Fryer Veggie Frittata

Servings: 2 | **Prep Time:** 5 min | **Cook Time:** 12 min

Ingredients:

- 4 large eggs
- ¼ cup spinach, chopped
- ¼ cup bell peppers, diced (any color)
- ¼ cup onions, diced
- ¼ cup low-fat cheese, shredded (optional)
- ¼ teaspoon salt
- ¼ teaspoon black pepper
- Cooking spray or a little olive oil

Instructions:

1. Spray a small oven-safe dish or cake pan that fits in your air fryer with cooking spray or lightly brush with olive oil.
2. In a medium bowl, whisk together the eggs, salt, and pepper. Add the spinach, bell peppers, onions, and cheese (if using), and stir to combine.
3. Pour the egg mixture into the prepared dish. Place the dish in the air fryer basket and cook at 350°F (175°C) for 10-12 minutes, or until the eggs are fully set and the top is golden brown.
4. Let the frittata cool for a minute before slicing. Serve warm.

Breakfast Tacos

Servings: 2 | **Prep Time:** 5 min | **Cook Time:** 10 min

Ingredients:

- 4 large eggs
- 2 low-carb tortillas
- ½ avocado, sliced
- ¼ cup spinach, chopped
- ¼ cup bell peppers, diced (any color)
- ¼ cup onions, diced
- 1 tablespoon olive oil
- Salt and pepper to taste
- Optional toppings: salsa, shredded cheese, hot sauce, or cilantro

Instructions:

1. Preheat the air fryer to 350°F (175°C). Toss the spinach, bell peppers, and onions in olive oil. Place the veggies in an air fryer-safe pan or on a piece of aluminum foil in the basket. Cook for 5 minutes, stirring halfway through.
2. In a bowl, whisk the eggs with salt and pepper. Pour the eggs over the cooked veggies in the air fryer basket and cook for another 5-6 minutes, stirring halfway through until scrambled and set.
3. While the eggs are cooking, place the low-carb tortillas in the air fryer for 1-2 minutes to warm them up.
4. Divide the scrambled eggs and veggies between the two tortillas. Top each with avocado slices and any optional toppings like salsa, shredded cheese, or hot sauce.
5. Fold the tortillas and enjoy your breakfast tacos warm.

Tips & Tricks:

- **Meal Prep:** The frittata can be stored in the fridge for up to 3 days. Simply reheat in the air fryer or microwave before serving.
- **Substitution Suggestions:** You can substitute or add other vegetables like mushrooms, zucchini, or cherry tomatoes. For a dairy-free option, omit the cheese or use a dairy-free alternative.
- **Blood Sugar Management:** This high-protein, low-carb meal is perfect for keeping blood sugar levels stable and providing sustained energy.

NUTRITION: Calories 170 | Carbs 4g | Protein 14g | Fat 11g | Fiber 1g | Sugar 2g

Tips & Tricks:

- **Meal Prep:** You can cook the eggs and veggies ahead of time and store them in the fridge for up to 3 days. Reheat in the air fryer and assemble the tacos when ready to eat.
- **Substitution Suggestions:** Use dairy-free cheese or swap the avocado for guacamole. For a protein boost, add cooked turkey bacon or sausage crumbles.
- **Blood Sugar Management:** Low-carb tortillas combined with eggs and healthy fats from avocado help keep blood sugar levels stable and provide a filling, balanced meal.

NUTRITION: Calories 300 | Carbs 10g | Protein 16g | Fat 22g | Fiber 7g | Sugar 2g

Cauliflower Hash Browns with Eggs

Servings: 2 | **Prep Time:** 10 min | **Cook Time:** 15 min

Ingredients:

For the Cauliflower Hash Browns:
- 1 ½ cups cauliflower rice (store-bought or grated from fresh cauliflower)
- 1 large egg
- ¼ cup shredded low-fat cheese (cheddar or mozzarella)
- ¼ cup almond flour
- ½ teaspoon garlic powder
- ¼ teaspoon salt
- ¼ teaspoon black pepper
- Cooking spray or a little olive oil

For the Eggs:
- 2 large eggs (cooked your way: scrambled, fried, or poached)

Instructions:

1. In a bowl, mix the cauliflower rice, egg, cheese, almond flour, garlic powder, salt, and black pepper until combined.
2. Form the mixture into small patties (about 4-5 patties total).
3. Spray the air fryer basket with cooking spray or brush with a little olive oil. Place the cauliflower patties in the basket and cook at 375°F (190°C) for 12-15 minutes, flipping halfway through, until golden brown and crispy on the outside.
4. While the hash browns are cooking, prepare your eggs to your liking (scrambled, fried, or poached) on the stovetop or in the air fryer.
5. Serve the crispy cauliflower hash browns alongside your cooked eggs. Add a sprinkle of extra cheese or hot sauce if desired.

Cinnamon «Toast» Bites

Servings: 2 | **Prep Time:** 5 min | **Cook Time:** 5 min

Ingredients:
- 2 slices low-carb bread
- 1 tablespoon butter or coconut oil, melted
- 1 teaspoon ground cinnamon
- 1 teaspoon sugar substitute (like erythritol or stevia)
- Cooking spray (optional)

Instructions:

1. Cut the low-carb bread into bite-sized squares (about 9 pieces per slice).
2. In a small bowl, mix the melted butter or coconut oil with cinnamon and sugar substitute until combined.
3. Lightly brush or toss the bread squares with the cinnamon mixture, making sure they are evenly coated.
4. Place the bread squares in the air fryer basket in a single layer. Air fry at 350°F (175°C) for 4-5 minutes, shaking the basket halfway through, until the toast bites are crispy and golden.
5. Let the cinnamon toast bites cool slightly before serving. Enjoy warm!

Tips & Tricks:

- **Meal Prep:** The cauliflower mixture can be made in advance and stored in the fridge for up to 2 days. Simply form the patties and air fry when ready to serve.
- **Substitution Suggestions:** Swap almond flour for coconut flour if needed, but use only 2 tablespoons. For dairy-free, use a dairy-free cheese alternative or omit the cheese.
- **Blood Sugar Management:** Cauliflower is low in carbs and high in fiber, making it an excellent replacement for traditional potatoes in hash browns. This meal, combined with protein-rich eggs, helps maintain stable blood sugar levels.

Tips & Tricks:

- **Meal Prep:** You can pre-cut the bread and store it in an airtight container for quick assembly in the mornings. Just coat with the cinnamon mixture and air fry when ready.
- **Substitution Suggestions:** You can use ghee or a vegan butter substitute for a dairy-free option. If desired, add a pinch of vanilla extract to the cinnamon mixture for added flavor.
- **Blood Sugar Management:** Using low-carb bread and a sugar substitute helps keep this snack or breakfast treat diabetic-friendly while still satisfying a sweet craving.

NUTRITION: Calories 250 | Carbs 8g | Protein 16g | Fat 17g | Fiber 4g | Sugar 2g

NUTRITION: Calories 180 | Carbs 6g | Protein 5g | Fat 15g | Fiber 4g | Sugar 0g

Bagels with Cream Cheese and Smoked Salmon

Servings: 2 | **Prep Time:** 10 min | **Cook Time:** 12 min

Ingredients:

For the Bagels:
- 1 cup almond flour
- 1 ½ cups shredded mozzarella cheese
- 2 tablespoons cream cheese
- 1 large egg, beaten
- 1 teaspoon baking powder
- ¼ teaspoon garlic powder (optional)
- ¼ teaspoon salt
- Cooking spray or a little olive oil

For Serving:
- 2 tablespoons cream cheese
- 2 oz smoked salmon
- Optional toppings: capers, sliced red onions, dill, or lemon wedges

Instructions:

1. In a microwave-safe bowl, melt the mozzarella cheese and cream cheese together in the microwave for 1-2 minutes, stirring halfway through, until fully melted and combined.
2. In a separate bowl, mix almond flour, baking powder, garlic powder (if using), and salt. Add the melted cheese mixture and beaten egg to the dry ingredients, and knead the dough until smooth and well combined.
3. Divide the dough into 2 equal portions and shape each into a bagel (donut shape). Spray the air fryer basket with cooking spray or brush with olive oil. Place the bagels in the air fryer basket.
4. Cook the bagels in the air fryer at 350°F (175°C) for 10-12 minutes or until golden brown and firm.
5. Let the bagels cool slightly before slicing them in half. Spread each half with cream cheese and top with smoked salmon. Add optional toppings like capers, red onions, or dill if desired.

Tips & Tricks:

- **Meal Prep:** You can prepare the keto bagels ahead of time and store them in the fridge for up to 3 days. Reheat in the air fryer or toaster oven before serving.
- **Substitution Suggestions:** Use dairy-free cream cheese or vegan cheese if needed. For extra flavor, sprinkle the bagels with sesame seeds or everything bagel seasoning before air frying.
- **Blood Sugar Management:** Almond flour is low in carbs and high in healthy fats, making these keto bagels an excellent choice for a satisfying, blood sugar-friendly breakfast or snack.

NUTRITION: Calories 450 | Carbs 8g | Protein 25g | Fat 38g | Fiber 4g | Sugar 2g

Breakfast Egg Rolls

Servings: 2 | **Prep Time:** 10 min | **Cook Time:** 10 min

Ingredients:
- 4 large eggs
- ½ cup spinach, chopped
- 2 turkey sausage links, cooked and crumbled
- ¼ cup shredded low-fat cheese (optional)
- 4 low-carb egg roll wrappers
- Cooking spray or a little olive oil
- Salt and pepper to taste
- Optional: hot sauce or salsa for dipping

Instructions:

1. In a skillet, cook the eggs over medium heat, scrambling them until just set. Add spinach and cooked turkey sausage, and season with salt and pepper. Cook for 1-2 more minutes until the spinach wilts slightly. Remove from heat.
2. Lay the egg roll wrappers on a clean surface. Evenly divide the egg mixture and place it in the center of each wrapper. Add a sprinkle of cheese if using. Fold the bottom corner of the wrapper over the filling, fold in the sides, and roll tightly. Use a little water to seal the edges.
3. Preheat the air fryer to 375°F (190°C). Spray the egg rolls with cooking spray or lightly brush with olive oil. Place them in the air fryer basket, seam side down, and cook for 8-10 minutes, flipping halfway through, until golden and crispy.
4. Serve warm with optional dipping sauces like hot sauce or salsa.

Tips & Tricks:

- **Meal Prep:** You can assemble the egg rolls ahead of time and store them in the fridge for up to 24 hours. Air fry them just before serving for a fresh, crispy texture.
- **Substitution Suggestions:** Use a vegetarian sausage or omit the sausage for a vegetarian version. You can also use dairy-free cheese if needed.
- **Blood Sugar Management:** Low-carb egg roll wrappers and a protein-rich filling make these breakfast egg rolls a great way to start the day without spiking blood sugar levels.

NUTRITION: Calories 300 | Carbs 12g | Protein 24g | Fat 17g | Fiber 2g | Sugar 1g

Scrambled Egg Muffins

Servings: 2 | **Prep Time:** 5 min | **Cook Time:** 15 min

Ingredients:

- 4 large eggs
- ¼ cup spinach, chopped
- ¼ cup bell peppers, diced (any color)
- ¼ cup shredded low-fat cheese (optional)
- ¼ cup cooked and crumbled turkey bacon (optional for meat option)
- ¼ teaspoon salt
- ¼ teaspoon black pepper
- Cooking spray or a little olive oil

Instructions:

1. Spray silicone muffin molds or an air fryer-safe muffin tray with cooking spray or lightly brush with olive oil.
2. In a medium bowl, whisk the eggs, salt, and pepper until fully combined. Stir in the spinach, bell peppers, cheese, and turkey bacon (if using).
3. Evenly divide the egg mixture into the muffin molds.
4. Place the molds in the air fryer basket and cook at 350°F (175°C) for 12-15 minutes, or until the eggs are fully set and slightly golden on top.
5. Let the muffins cool for a minute before removing them from the molds. Serve warm.

Tips & Tricks:

- **Meal Prep:** These muffins can be stored in the fridge for up to 3 days. Simply reheat in the air fryer or microwave before serving.
- **Substitution Suggestions:** For a dairy-free option, skip the cheese or use a dairy-free cheese alternative. You can also swap turkey bacon for chicken sausage or omit the meat for a vegetarian version.
- **Blood Sugar Management:** High in protein and low in carbs, these muffins are ideal for keeping blood sugar levels stable throughout the morning.

NUTRITION: Calories 190 | Carbs 3g | Protein 15g | Fat 13g | Fiber 1g | Sugar 2g

Shakshuka

Servings: 2 | **Prep Time:** 5 min | **Cook Time:** 15 min

Ingredients:

- 4 large eggs
- ½ cup diced tomatoes (canned or fresh)
- ¼ cup bell peppers, diced
- ¼ cup onions, diced
- 1 clove garlic, minced
- ½ teaspoon cumin
- ½ teaspoon paprika
- ¼ teaspoon chili flakes (optional for heat)
- Salt and pepper to taste
- 1 tablespoon olive oil
- Fresh parsley or cilantro for garnish (optional)

Instructions:

1. Preheat the air fryer to 350°F (175°C). In an air fryer-safe pan or dish, add olive oil, garlic, onions, and bell peppers. Air fry for 4-5 minutes until softened.
2. Stir in the diced tomatoes, cumin, paprika, chili flakes (if using), salt, and pepper. Air fry for another 4-5 minutes, stirring halfway through, until the sauce thickens slightly.
3. Create small wells in the tomato sauce and carefully crack an egg into each well. Return the dish to the air fryer and cook at 350°F (175°C) for 6-8 minutes, or until the eggs are cooked to your liking (with runny or fully set yolks).
4. Garnish with fresh parsley or cilantro if desired. Serve warm with a side of whole grain bread or low-carb pita.

Tips & Tricks:

- **Meal Prep:** The tomato sauce can be made in advance and stored in the fridge for up to 2 days. When ready, simply reheat the sauce and add the eggs to cook.
- **Substitution Suggestions:** You can add other veggies like zucchini or mushrooms to the sauce for extra flavor and nutrients. For more spice, increase the chili flakes or add a dash of hot sauce.
- **Blood Sugar Management:** Shakshuka is a low-carb, nutrient-dense dish with healthy fats and protein that help stabilize blood sugar levels, making it a great breakfast or brunch option.

NUTRITION: Calories 220 | Carbs 8g | Protein 12g | Fat 16g | Fiber 2g | Sugar 4g

Stuffed Zucchini Boats

Servings: 2 | **Prep Time:** 10 min | **Cook Time:** 12 min

Ingredients:

- 2 medium zucchinis
- 3 large eggs
- ¼ cup bell peppers, diced
- ¼ cup onions, diced
- ¼ cup spinach, chopped
- ¼ cup low-fat shredded cheese (optional)
- 1 tablespoon olive oil
- Salt and pepper to taste
- Cooking spray or a little olive oil

Instructions:

1. Slice the zucchinis in half lengthwise and scoop out the center using a spoon to create «boats.» Drizzle the zucchini boats with olive oil and season with a little salt and pepper.
2. In a bowl, whisk the eggs with salt and pepper. In a skillet, sauté the bell peppers, onions, and spinach in a little olive oil until softened, about 3-4 minutes. Add the whisked eggs to the skillet and scramble until just set.
3. Evenly divide the scrambled eggs and veggie mixture into the hollowed-out zucchini boats. Top with shredded cheese if using.
4. Spray the air fryer basket with cooking spray. Place the stuffed zucchini boats in the air fryer basket and cook at 375°F (190°C) for 10-12 minutes, or until the zucchini is tender and the cheese is melted and golden.
5. Let cool for a minute before serving. Enjoy warm!

Tempeh Breakfast Hash (Vegan)

Servings: 2 | **Prep Time:** 10 min | **Cook Time:** 15 min

Ingredients:

- 4 oz tempeh, diced
- 1 medium sweet potato, diced
- ½ cup bell peppers, diced (any color)
- ¼ cup onions, diced
- 1 tablespoon olive oil
- ½ teaspoon smoked paprika
- ½ teaspoon garlic powder
- Salt and pepper to taste
- Fresh parsley for garnish (optional)
- Cooking spray or a little olive oil

Instructions:

1. Preheat the air fryer to 375°F (190°C). Toss the diced sweet potatoes with olive oil, smoked paprika, garlic powder, salt, and pepper. Place them in the air fryer basket and cook for 10 minutes, shaking the basket halfway through.
2. After 10 minutes, add the diced tempeh, bell peppers, and onions to the air fryer basket with the sweet potatoes. Toss everything together, then air fry for an additional 5-7 minutes, or until the tempeh is golden and the veggies are tender.
3. Garnish the hash with fresh parsley if desired. Serve warm as a standalone meal or alongside a slice of whole-grain toast.

Tips & Tricks:

- **Meal Prep:** You can prepare the filling in advance and store it in the fridge for up to 2 days. When ready, stuff the zucchini and air fry.
- **Substitution Suggestions:** For a dairy-free option, skip the cheese or use a dairy-free cheese alternative. Add extra veggies like mushrooms or tomatoes for more flavor and nutrients.
- **Blood Sugar Management:** Zucchini is low in carbs and rich in fiber, making this meal perfect for those managing blood sugar. Pair with a small side salad for a well-rounded breakfast or lunch.

Tips & Tricks:

- **Meal Prep:** This hash can be prepped in advance and stored in the fridge for up to 3 days. Reheat in the air fryer or microwave before serving.
- **Substitution Suggestions:** You can swap sweet potatoes for regular potatoes or add more veggies like zucchini or mushrooms. For extra flavor, drizzle with hot sauce or a squeeze of lime.
- **Blood Sugar Management:** Sweet potatoes are high in fiber and provide slow-digesting carbs, making this a filling and blood sugar-friendly meal, while tempeh offers plant-based protein.

NUTRITION: Calories 230 | Carbs 7g | Protein 14g | Fat 17g | Fiber 2g | Sugar 3g

NUTRITION: Calories 280 | Carbs 28g | Protein 12g | Fat 13g | Fiber 6g | Sugar 6g

Spinach and Feta Omelette

Servings: 2 | **Prep Time:** 5 min | **Cook Time:** 10 min

Ingredients:
- 4 large eggs
- ½ cup fresh spinach, chopped
- ¼ cup feta cheese, crumbled
- 1 tablespoon olive oil
- ¼ teaspoon salt
- ¼ teaspoon black pepper
- Cooking spray or a little olive oil

Instructions:
1. Preheat the air fryer to 350°F (175°C). Lightly spray an air fryer-safe dish or small pan with cooking spray.
2. In a medium bowl, whisk the eggs with salt and pepper. Stir in the chopped spinach and crumbled feta cheese.
3. Pour the egg mixture into the prepared dish. Place the dish in the air fryer basket and cook for 8-10 minutes, or until the omelette is set and the edges are golden.
4. Let the omelette cool for a minute before slicing. Serve warm with a side salad or whole grain toast if desired.

Tips & Tricks:
- **Meal Prep:** This omelette can be made in advance and stored in the fridge for up to 2 days. Reheat in the air fryer or microwave before serving.
- **Substitution Suggestions:** Swap feta cheese for goat cheese or a dairy-free alternative if needed. Add extra Mediterranean flavors by incorporating sun-dried tomatoes or olives.
- **Blood Sugar Management:** Eggs are an excellent source of protein, and combined with the healthy fats from olive oil and feta, this low-carb meal helps keep blood sugar levels stable.

NUTRITION: Calories 240 | Carbs 2g | Protein 15g | Fat 19g | Fiber 1g | Sugar 1g

Breakfast Pizza

Servings: 2 | **Prep Time:** 10 min | **Cook Time:** 12 min

Ingredients:
For the Low-Carb Crust:
- ½ cup almond flour
- 1 large egg
- ½ cup shredded mozzarella cheese
- ¼ teaspoon baking powder
- ¼ teaspoon garlic powder (optional)
- Salt and pepper to taste

For the Toppings:
- 2 large eggs
- 2 slices turkey bacon, cooked and crumbled
- ¼ cup shredded low-fat cheese (cheddar or mozzarella)
- 1 tablespoon olive oil
- Salt and pepper to taste
- Fresh herbs for garnish (optional)

Instructions:
1. In a medium bowl, mix the almond flour, egg, shredded mozzarella, baking powder, garlic powder, salt, and pepper until well combined. Form the mixture into a round pizza shape (about 6 inches in diameter).
2. Preheat the air fryer to 350°F (175°C). Place the crust in the air fryer basket on a piece of parchment paper. Air fry for 5-6 minutes until golden and firm.
3. Crack the eggs directly onto the crust (or scramble them first if you prefer). Sprinkle the crumbled turkey bacon and shredded cheese evenly over the pizza. Return the pizza to the air fryer and cook for another 6-7 minutes, or until the eggs are set and the cheese is melted.
4. Let the breakfast pizza cool slightly before slicing. Garnish with fresh herbs if desired. Serve warm.

Tips & Tricks:
- **Meal Prep:** The crust can be made ahead of time and stored in the fridge for up to 3 days. When ready, just add the toppings and air fry.
- **Substitution Suggestions:** For a vegetarian option, omit the turkey bacon and add veggies like spinach, mushrooms, or bell peppers. You can also use a dairy-free cheese alternative if needed.
- **Blood Sugar Management:** This low-carb, high-protein pizza helps stabilize blood sugar levels, making it an ideal breakfast choice for diabetics.

NUTRITION: Calories 350 | Carbs 6g | Protein 22g | Fat 27g | Fiber 3g | Sugar 1g

Tofu Scramble (Vegan)

Servings: 2 | **Prep Time:** 5 min | **Cook Time:** 10 min

Ingredients:

- ½ block (7 oz) firm tofu, crumbled
- ½ cup bell peppers, diced (any color)
- ¼ cup onions, diced
- ¼ cup spinach, chopped
- 1 tablespoon olive oil
- ½ teaspoon turmeric powder
- ¼ teaspoon garlic powder
- ¼ teaspoon paprika
- Salt and pepper to taste
- Cooking spray or a little olive oil

Instructions:

1. Crumble the tofu into small pieces and set aside. In a medium bowl, toss the tofu with turmeric, garlic powder, paprika, salt, and pepper until evenly coated.
2. Preheat the air fryer to 350°F (175°C). Toss the diced bell peppers, onions, and spinach with olive oil, then place the vegetables in an air fryer-safe pan or directly in the air fryer basket. Cook for 5 minutes, stirring halfway through.
3. After 5 minutes, add the seasoned tofu to the veggies in the air fryer. Cook for another 5 minutes, stirring halfway through, until the tofu is lightly crispy and golden.
4. Let the tofu scramble cool for a minute, then serve warm. Garnish with fresh herbs or hot sauce if desired.

Tips & Tricks:

- **Meal Prep:** The tofu scramble can be made ahead of time and stored in the fridge for up to 3 days. Reheat in the air fryer or microwave before serving.
- **Substitution Suggestions:** You can add more veggies like mushrooms, zucchini, or cherry tomatoes. For extra flavor, squeeze some fresh lemon juice over the scramble before serving.
- **Blood Sugar Management:** Tofu is low in carbs and high in protein, making it an excellent choice for maintaining stable blood sugar levels, while the veggies add fiber and nutrients.

NUTRITION: Calories 180 | Carbs 6g | Protein 12g | Fat 13g | Fiber 2g | Sugar 2g

Portobello Mushroom Breakfast Bites

Servings: 2 | **Prep Time:** 5 min | **Cook Time:** 12 min

Ingredients:

- 2 large Portobello mushrooms, stems removed and cleaned
- 3 large eggs
- ½ cup fresh spinach, chopped
- ¼ cup low-fat shredded cheese (optional)
- 1 tablespoon olive oil
- ¼ teaspoon salt
- ¼ teaspoon black pepper
- Cooking spray or a little olive oil

Instructions:

1. Preheat the air fryer to 350°F (175°C). Spread a small amount of olive oil on the Portobello mushrooms and season with salt and pepper. Set aside.
2. In a medium skillet, cook the eggs with spinach over medium heat, scrambling them until just set. Season with salt and pepper. Remove from heat and stir in the cheese if using.
3. Divide the scrambled egg mixture evenly between the two Portobello mushrooms, stuffing them generously.
4. Place the stuffed mushrooms in the air fryer basket. Cook for 8-10 minutes, or until the mushrooms are tender and the filling is heated through.
5. Let the stuffed mushrooms cool for a minute before serving. Enjoy warm.

Tips & Tricks:

- **Meal Prep:** You can prepare the stuffed mushrooms in advance and store them in the fridge for up to 1 day. Reheat in the air fryer before serving.
- **Substitution Suggestions:** For a dairy-free version, omit the cheese or use a dairy-free alternative. You can also add other vegetables like bell peppers or tomatoes to the egg mixture.
- **Blood Sugar Management:** Portobello mushrooms are low in carbs and provide a healthy base for this high-protein, low-carb breakfast, helping to keep blood sugar levels stable.

NUTRITION: Calories 220 | Carbs 5g | Protein 13g | Fat 17g | Fiber 2g | Sugar 2g

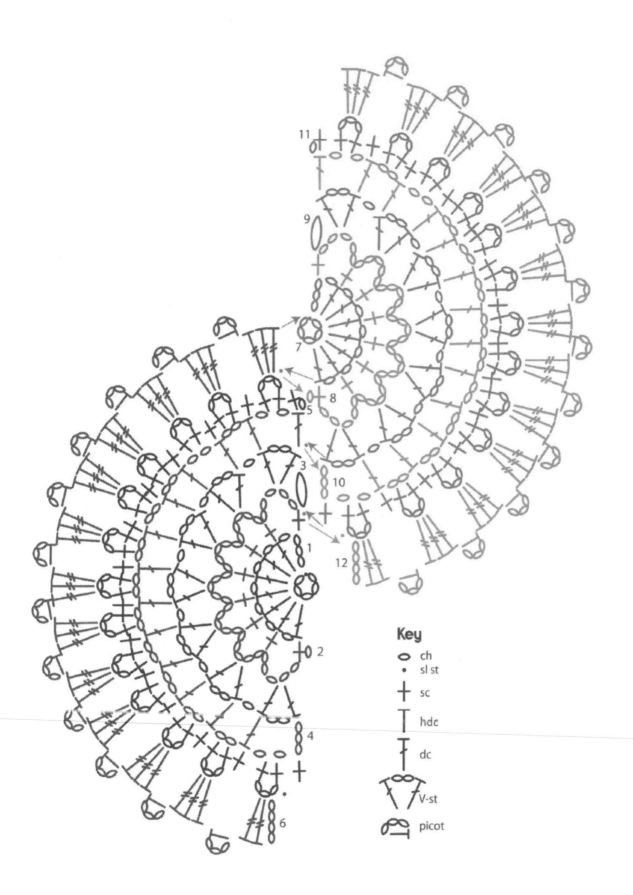

Key

⬯	ch
•	sl st
+	sc
⊤	hdc
⊤	dc
⋏	V-st
◠	picot

pentagon
mitts

A five-sided polygon motif is the basis for these clever mitts. Make the motifs that adorn the palm and back of the hand, then add finishing rows. You'll welcome an abundance of warmth and color with this variegated sock yarn.

finished size

Size Small; 3½ × 8½" (9 × 21.5 cm) when flat; 5" (12.5 cm) at widest point.

yarn

166 yards (152 m), sock weight (#1 Super Fine).

Shown here: Patons Kroy Socks FX (75% washable wool, 25% nylon; 166 yd [152 m]/1.75 oz [50 g]): #243457 Celestial Colors, 1 skein.

hook

Size H/8 (5 mm).

Adjust hook size if necessary to obtain correct gauge.

notions

3 locking stitch markers (m), yarn needle.

gauge

Rnds 1–4 = 4" (10 cm), point to point.

notes

Mitts can be made larger as follows: For Size Medium only: Turn and repeat Row 1, one time. For Size Large only: Turn and repeat Row 1, two times.

All rounds are worked on the right side without turning. After the hand sections, the hand sides are seamed and the wrist section is added.

Reserve 3" (7.5 cm) per single crochet (plus slip knot and tail) for seaming. (Mitts in photo are whipstitched.) Whipstitching takes the least amount of yarn if you're short on fiber.

Written instructions and stitch diagrams are provided. Use either type alone, or both together as needed.

Special Stitches

Beginning 3 Double Crochet Cluster (beg-3-dc-cl)

Ch 3, yo, insert hook in indicated st, yo and pull up lp, yo, draw through 2 lps on hook, yo, insert hook in same st, yo and pull up lp, yo, draw through 2 lps on hook, draw through all 3 lps on hook.

3 Double Crochet Cluster (3-dc-cl)

[Yo, insert hook in indicated st, yo, pull up a lp, yo, pull through 2 lps on hook] 3 times, yo, pull through all 4 lps on hook.

The General Plan

Instead of splitting the ball in two before you begin working, work the two items at the same time. For these mitts, there is a palm side and a back-of-hand side, and then they are seamed. Work the hand portion for each mitt, then you can use up the remaining yarn by adding more rows, alternating working on one mitt then adding rows to the other mitt until the yarn is gone and the mitts are equal.

Hand Section 1 (make 2)

One will be used for the palm of the right hand and the other will be used for the back of the left hand.

Make an adjustable ring (see Glossary).

Rnd 1: (RS) Beg-3-dc-cl (see Special Stitches) in ring, (ch 3, 3-dc-cl [see Special Stitches] in ring) 4 times, ch 1; join with hdc in first cl, do not turn—5 3-dc-cl.

Rnd 2: (RS) Ch 1, sc in same sp as join, [(sc, ch 3, sc) in next 3-dc-cl, (sc, ch 5, sc) in ch-3 sp] 4 times, (sc, ch 3, sc) in next 3-dc-cl, (sc, ch 2) in first ch-3 sp; join with dc in first sc, do not turn—5 ch-5 corner sps, 5 ch-3 sps.

Rnd 3: (RS) Beg-3-dc-cl in sp created by dc join, [ch 1, 3 hdc in ch-3 sp, ch 1, (3-dc-cl, ch 3, 3-dc-cl) in next ch-5 sp] 4 times, ch 1, 3 hdc in ch-3 sp, ch 1, 3-dc-cl in joining dc, ch 1; join with hdc in first 3-dc-cl, do not turn—10 3-dc-cl, 15 hdc.

Rnd 4: (RS) Ch 1, 2 sc in same sp as join, sc in next 3-dc-cl, sc in ch-1 sp, sc in each of next 3 hdc, sc in next ch-1 sp, sc in 3-dc-cl, [5 sc in next ch-3 corner sp, sc in next 3-dc-cl, sc in next ch-1 sp, sc in each of next 3 hdc, sc in next ch-1 sp, sc in next 3-dc-cl] 4 times, 3 sc in last corner sp; join with sl st in first sc, do not turn, do not fasten off—60 sc.

Switch to working in turned rows. Rows do not go all the way around the perimeter.

Note: Row 1 works 3 sides only.

Row 1: (RS) Ch 1 (does not count as a st), dc in same st as join, dc in each of next 10 sc, 3 dc in middle sc of 5-sc corner group, dc in each of next 11 sc, 3 dc in next sc in middle sc of 5-sc corner group, dc in next 12 sc, TURN, leaving remaining stitches unworked—40 dc.

Note: For smaller hands, you can change all the double crochets to single crochets. For larger hands, you can change all the double crochets to treble crochets, but it will use more yarn, so your wrist portion may have to be shorter to compensate.

Row 2: (WS) Ch 1, sc in each of next 13 sts, 3 sc in middle dc of 3-dc group, sc in each of next 13 sts, TURN, leaving remaining sides unworked—29 sc.

These two sides that have the extra single crochets make up the thumb edge and the wrist edge. Fasten off.

Hand Section 1

Palm of Right Hand/Back of Left Hand

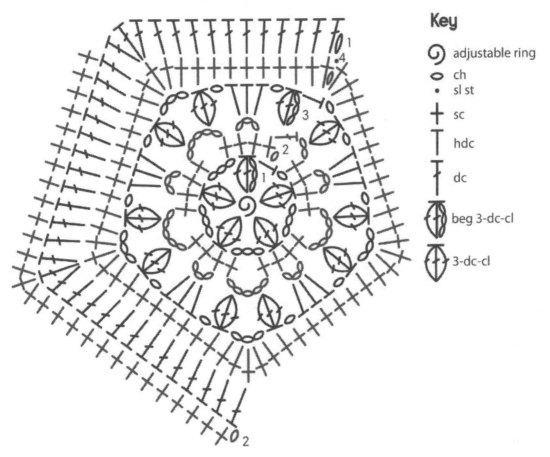

Key

ʕ	adjustable ring
○	ch
•	sl st
†	sc
T	hdc
╪	dc
◈	beg 3-dc-cl
◈	3-dc-cl

Hand Section 2 (make 2)

These are the same as for the Hand Section 1 above. One will be used for the back of the right hand and the other will be used for the palm of the left hand.

Note: The right sides should always be facing outward and the extra rows of single crochet go along the thumb and wrist.

Work same as Hand Section 1 through Rnd 4.

Note: Row 1 works 3 sides only.

Row 1: (RS) Ch 1 (does not count as a st), dc in same st, pm in the first dc, dc in next 10 sc, 3 dc in middle sc of 5-sc corner group, dc in next 11 sc, 3 dc in middle sc of 5-sc corner group, dc in next 12 sc, leave remaining stitches unworked. Fasten off—40 dc.

Note: For smaller hands, you can change all the double crochets to single crochets. For larger hands, you can change all the double crochets to treble crochets, but doing so uses more yarn, so your wrist portion may have to be shorter to compensate.

Row 2: With RS facing; join new yarn with sc in the marked st of Row 1, remove the marker, sc in the next 11 sts, 3 sc in middle dc of 3-dc group, sc in each of the next 14 sts, TURN, leaving remaining sides unworked—29 sc.

These two sides that have the extra single crochets make up the thumb edge and wrist edge. Fasten off.

Hand Section 2

Palm of Left Hand/Back of Right Hand

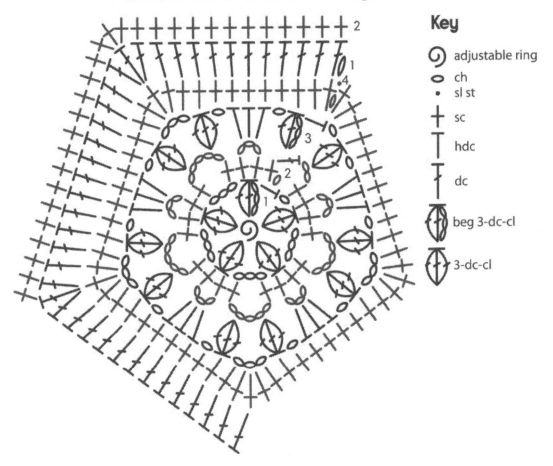

Key

- 🌀 adjustable ring
- ⬭ ch
- • sl st
- ✝ sc
- ⊤ hdc
- ✝ dc
- beg 3-dc-cl
- 3-dc-cl

Seam the Two Hand Pieces

With right sides facing each other, seam by whipstitching them along thumb edge toward wrist. Cut yarn and seam down small finger side toward wrist.

Seam gap between thumb and index finger for 11 sts. If needed, try them on and pin the seam in place with locking stitch markers before seaming.

Turn right sides out.

Wrist Section

Rnd 1: Join new yarn with RS facing with dc in the side seam under the thumb, dc in each of the next 29 sts; join with sl st in first dc, do not turn—30 dc.

Note: Try on the mitts. You can increase as needed by placing 2 dc in one stitch. Whatever you do on one mitt, repeat for the other.

To use up the yarn efficiently, work 2 wrist rnds on one mitt then 2 rnds on the other until you run out of yarn and the mitts are even. You can work from both outside and inside the ball at the same time to avoid cutting the yarn and rejoining.

Rnd 2: Ch 1, dc in same st as join and in each st around; join with sl st in first dc, do not turn—30 dc.

Rnds 3–desired length (shown mitts have 10 rnds): Ch 1 (does not count as a st), dc in first st, [FPdc in next st, dc in next st] 14 times, FPdc in next st; join with sl st in first dc, do not turn—30 sts.

Final Rnd: Sl st in each st around. Fasten off.

Sl st around finger opening if desired: With RS facing; join new yarn with sl st in any st and sl st in every st around. Fasten off.

Repeat for second mitt.

Finishing

Weave in ends.

handled
purse

Texture bursts from the surface with dimensional popcorn stitches. Easy hexagonal motifs are joined as they are worked for a no-sew bag body! The handles are crocheted on as the edging is worked for a quick and dramatic finish.

finished size

12" (30.5 cm) wide at base (with corners tucked in), 10½" (26.5 cm) wide at top at opening, 7¾" (19.5 cm) tall.

yarn

170 yards (156 m), worsted weight (#4 Medium).

Shown here: Lion Brand Vanna's Choice (100% acrylic; 170 yd [156 m]/3.5 oz [100g]): #105 Silver Blue, 1 skein.

hook

Size J/10 (6 mm).

Adjust hook size if necessary to obtain correct gauge.

notions

1 pair Blumenthal Purse n-alize-it! bead handbag handles measuring 6.125 × 4.75" (15.5 × 12 cm), yarn needle.

gauge

One motif = 4" (10 cm), point to point.

notes

You will first crochet three vertical rows of motifs, then add the sides.

Written instructions and stitch diagrams are provided. Use either type alone, or both together as needed.

Special Stitches

Beginning Popcorn (beg pc)

Ch 3 (counts as first dc), 2 dc in same sp, remove hook from lp, insert empty hook in the top 2 lps of the first dc/ch 3 of the group, insert the hook also in abandoned working lp, pull the working lp through the top of the first st.

Popcorn (pc)

Place 3 dc in indicated st or sp, remove hook from lp, insert empty hook in the top 2 lps of the first dc of the group, insert the hook also in abandoned working lp, pull the working lp through the top of the first st.

1st Motif

Make an adjustable ring (see Glossary).

Rnd 1: Beg pc (see Special Stitches) in ring, [ch 3, pc (see Special Stitches) in ring] 5 times, ch 3; join with sl st in beg pc—6 pc, 6 ch-3 sps.

Rnd 2: Sl st into ch-3 sp, ch 4 (counts as first tr), 4 more tr (see Glossary) in same sp, [ch 3, 5 tr in next ch-3 sp] 5 times, ch 3; join with sl st in top of first tr, fasten off—30 tr, 6 ch-3 sps.

2nd through 17th Motifs

Rnd 1: Rep Rnd 1 as for 1st Motif.

Rnd 2: Using the schematic on page 61 for guidance, sl st into ch-3 sp, ch 4 (counts as first tr), 4 more tr in same sp, [ch 1, sl st in ch-3 sp of previous motif as necessary, ch 1, 5 tr in next ch-3 sp] 5 times, ch 3; join with sl st in top of first tr, fasten off—30 tr, 6 ch-3 sps.

Top Edging and Handles

Join with single crochet through two lps on one thickness only along top edge. (If you're right-handed, join on the right and work with the bag public/right side facing and work toward the left; if you're left-handed, join on the left and work with the bag public/right side facing and work toward the right). Sc in each st, 3 sc in the ch-3 sps, 1 sc in ch-3 sp at the top edge, sc twice through the handle loops. Fasten off. Turn bag and repeat for second top edge and second handle. Fasten off and weave in ends.

Fold down the middle top motif and whipstitch it down. Repeat for the opposite one on the other side.

Tuck end corners 2" (5 cm) inward. With yarn and yarn needle, tack corners in their tucked position inside the bag.

Finishing

Weave in ends.

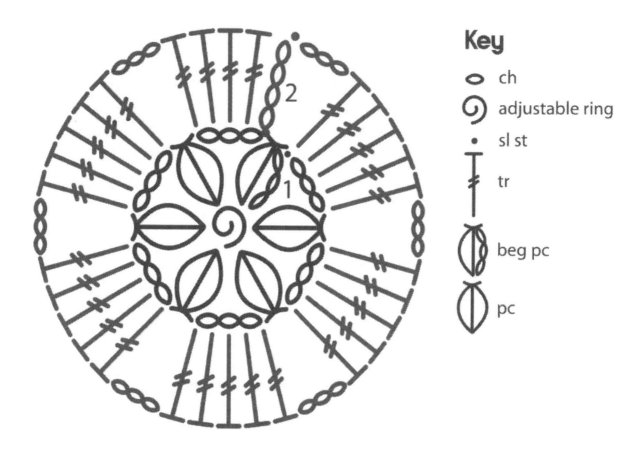

Key

- ch
- adjustable ring
- sl st
- tr
- beg pc
- pc

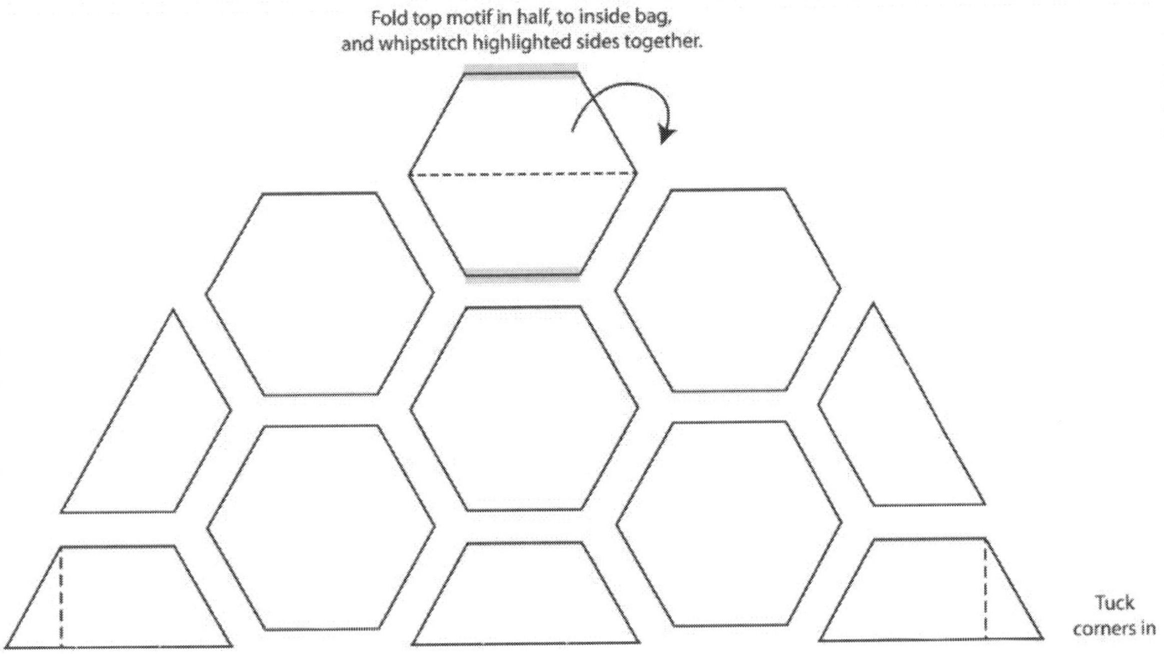

Fold top motif in half, to inside bag,
and whipstitch highlighted sides together.

Tuck
corners in

Schematic

greenery
hat

Texture is the crowning feature of this top-down hat. This design was inspired by the generous yardage of the yarn. Adding layering with the pattern maximizes the yarn and creates a thick but flexible finish. Made in superwash Merino wool, this hat will be warm and practical.

finished size

Fits 22" (56 cm) head; crown to brim (measured flat), 8" (20.5 cm).

yarn

186 yards (170 m), worsted weight (#4 Medium).

Shown here: Red Heart Chic Sheep by Marly Bird (100% Merino wool; 186 yd [170 m]/3.5 oz [100g]): #5632 Polo, 1 skein.

hook

Size I/9 (5.5 mm).

Adjust hook size if necessary to obtain correct gauge.

notions

Yarn needle.

gauge

Rnds 1–5 = 4" (10 cm).

notes

Throughout the pattern, the ch 1 at the beginning of a round does not count as a stitch.

Written instructions and stitch diagrams are provided. Use either type alone, or both together as needed.

The General Plan

Work from the crown to the brim until yarn runs out, allowing the hat to be as slouchy as needed to use the yarn completely. When using skeins that have generous yardage, layering stitches, as done in this project, helps use the yarn efficiently without leftovers.

Hat

Make an adjustable ring (see Glossary).

Rnd 1: (RS) h 3 (counts as a dc), 11 dc in ring; join with sl st in first dc—12 dc.

Rnd 2: Ch 1, sc in first st, FPdc (see Glossary) around same st, [sc in next st, FPdc around same st] 11 times; join with sl st in first sc—24 sts.

Rnd 3: Ch 1, sc in first st, *ch 5, sk 1 st, sc in next st; rep from * around, ch 5, sk 1 st; join with sl st in first sc—12 ch-5 lps.

Rnd 4: Working behind the ch-5 sps, ch 1 (does not count as a st), *3 tr (see Glossary) in skipped st 2 rnds previous, ch 1; rep from * around; join with sl st in first tr—36 tr, 12 ch-1 sps.

Rnd 5: Ch 1, sc in same st as join, *pulling up ch-5 lp from 2 rnds previous, sc through it and next tr on working rnd at the same time, sc in next tr, sc in ch-1 sp **, sc in next tr; rep from * around, ending last rep at **; join with sl st in first sc—48 sc.

Rnd 6: Ch 1 (does not count as a st), dc in same st, dc in each st around; join with sl st in first dc.

Rnd 7: Ch 1, sc in same st, *ch 5, sk 1 st, sc in next st; rep from * around, ch 5, sk 1 st; join with sl st in first sc.

Rnd 8: Ch 1 (does not count as a st), working behind the ch-5 sps, [3 tr in each skipped st 2 rnds previous] around; join with sl st in first tr—72 tr.

Rnd 9: Ch 1, sc in same st as join, *pulling up ch-5 lp from 2 rnds previous, sc through it and next tr on working rnd at the same time, sc in next 2 sts; rep from * around, ending last repeat with 1 sc; join with sl st in first sc—72 sc.

Rnds 10 and 11: Rep Rnds 6 and 7.

Rnd 12: Ch 1, [2 tr in each skipped st 2 rnds previous] around; join with sl st in first tr.

Rnd 13: Ch 1, sc in same st, *pulling up ch-5 lp from 2 rnds previous, sc through it and next tr on working rnd at the same time**, sc in next st; rep from * around , ending last rep at **; join with sl st in first sc—72 sc.

Rnds 14-25: [Rep Rnds 10-13] 3 times.

Rnd 26: Ch 1, *sc in each of the next 7 sts, sc2tog; rep from * around; join with sl st in first sc. Fasten off.

Finishing

Weave in ends.

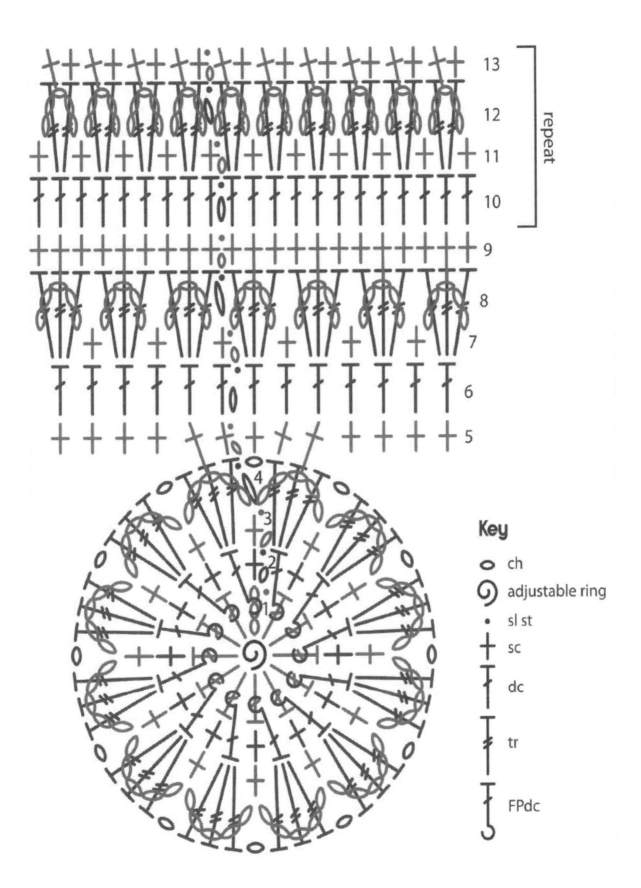

13

12 repeat

11

10

9

8

7

6

5

4

3

2

1

Key

⬭ ch

𖠋 adjustable ring

• sl st

✛ sc

✝ dc

𝆙 tr

𝅗 FPdc

star stitch
hat

Variegated yarns shine with the star stitch in this funky brim-up hat. Take the star stitch further with decreasing to create the perfect colorful beanie with amazing thickness and warmth. Eliminate the top few rounds to leave it open for a ponytail!

finished size

Fits 21½" (54.5 cm) head circumference; total height 9½" (24 cm).

yarn

197 yards (180 m), worsted weight (#4 Medium).

Shown here: Universal Yarn Classic Shades (70% acrylic, 30% wool; 197 yd [180 m]/3.5 oz [100g]): #711 Grapevine, 1 skein.

hook

Size I/9 (5.5 mm).

Adjust hook size if necessary to obtain correct gauge.

notions

Locking stitch marker (m), yarn needle.

gauge

8 stars and 10 rows = 4" (10 cm).

notes

Hat is worked from brim up toward crown.

Written instructions and stitch diagrams are provided.
Use either type alone, or both together as needed.

Special Stitches

Foundation Single Crochet (fsc)

First foundation single crochet: Ch 2, insert hook into 2nd ch from hook, yo, pull up a lp, yo, pull through 1 lp on hook (ch made), yo, pull through both lps on hook.

Next foundation single crochet: [Insert hook in last ch made, yo, pull up a lp, yo, pull through 1 lp on hook, yo, pull through both lps on hook] repeat as many times as indicated in instructions.

Star Stitch (star)

Insert hook into eyelet just formed, yo and draw up a lp, insert hook into final post st of last star made, yo and draw up a lp, insert hook into each of next 2 sts on row and draw up a lp (5 lps on hook), yo and pull through all lps on hook, ch 1 (eyelet made).

Star decrease (star dec)

Insert hook into eyelet just formed and draw up a lp, insert hook into final post st of last star made and draw up lp, insert hook into next st, sk 1 st, insert hook into next st on row and draw up a lp (5 lps on hook), yo and pull through all lps on hook, ch 1 (eyelet made).

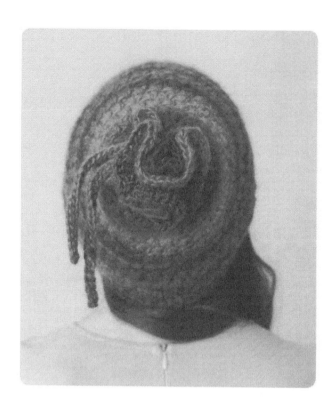

The General Plan

Starting at the brim, decrease until the desired slouchiness is reached. Add a fluffy few rows and tie for decoration. To use up more yarn, add more rounds by repeating Rnd 13.

Hat

Fsc (see Special Stitches) 83, taking care not to twist; join with sl st in first st to form a circle.

Rnd 1: (RS) Ch 2, work stars (see Special Stitches) all the way around, do not join at the end of Rnd 1. Mark first star with locking stitch marker and move up as work progresses—41 stars.

Rnds 2-7: Continue working in a spiral, make star using eyelets, top of beg ch-2, then next 2 sts.

Note: On Rnds 2-7, when working even, the last pull up of every star pulls up in an eyelet.

Rnd 8: *Work 3 stars, star dec (see Special Stitches) once; rep from * around, finish with 1 extra star—37 stars.

Rnd 9: Work even.

Rnd 10: Rep Rnd 8—33 stars.

Rnd 11: Work even.

Rnd 12: Rep Rnd 8—30 stars.

Rnd 13: Work even.

Rnd 14: Rep Rnd 8, finish with 3 extra stars—27 stars.

Rnd 15: Rep Rnd 8—24 stars.

Rnd 16: Rep Rnd 8, finish with 1 extra star—21 stars.

Rnd 17: *Work 2 stars, star dec once; rep around—18 stars.

Rnd 18: Rep Rnd 17, finish with 1 extra star—16 stars.

Rnd 19: Rep Rnd 17—11 stars.

Rnd 20: (Tie rnd) Ch 4 (counts as first dc plus ch-1 sp), *sk 1 st, dc in next st, ch 1; rep from * around; join with sl st in 3rd ch of beg ch-4 —11 dc, 11 ch-1 sps.

Rnd 21: Ch 1 (does not count as a st), working in front lp only, 3 dc in each ch and st around; join with sl st in first dc—66 dc.

Rnd 22: Ch 4 (counts as first tr), working in unused back lp only of Rnd 20, 2 tr in first st, 3 tr in each ch around; join with sl st in first tr— 66 tr.

Fasten off.

Weave in ends.

Tie

Ch 101, sl st in 2nd ch from hook and in each ch across—100 sl st.

Fasten off. Weave through ch-1 sps of Rnd 20. Tie in a bow.

Finishing

Edging: Join new yarn with sc in any stitch on brim under the foundation chain, *ch 1, sc in next st; rep from * around; join with sl st in first st. Fasten off.

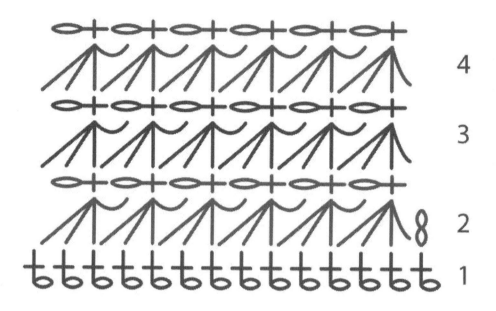

Key

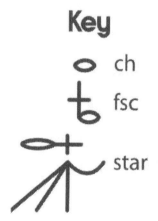

o   ch

fsc

star

horizontal slouch
hat

Eye-catching horizontal banding is created with a fun and easy slip stitch method and turned rows. The textural stripes add dimension in this rich solid yarn. This hat can be worn slouchy or has more of a beanie shape if the brim is turned up.

finished size

Fits 21" (53.5 cm) head circumference; crown to brim (measured flat), 9" (23 cm).

yarn

218 yards (199 m), worsted weight (#4 Medium).

Shown here: Berroco Vintage (52% acrylic, 40% wool, 8% nylon; 218 yd [199 m]/3.5 oz [100g]): #5173 Red Pepper, 1 skein.

hook

Size I/9 (5.5 mm).

Adjust hook size if necessary to obtain correct gauge.

notions

Locking stitch marker (m), yarn needle.

gauge

33 sts and 14 rows = 4" (10 cm) in pattern.

notes

Half the rounds are worked on the right side without turning. Some rows are turned and worked on the wrong side.

If you use the yarn listed in these instructions and achieve gauge, you'll only have 1 yard (91 cm) left over once finished, so don't feel nervous as you near the end of the pattern.

Written instructions and stitch diagrams are provided. Use either type alone, or both together as needed.

Special Stitches

Double Slip Stitch (dsst)

Double slip stitch is worked on the wrong side.

First st: Insert the hook in the first st, pull up a lp and leave it there, pull up a lp in the next st and pull it through the fabric and through all lps on the hook.

2nd and subsequent sts: Insert the hook in the last st that was just used, yo and pull up a lp through the fabric, insert the hook in the next unused st, yo and pull through the fabric and through all lps on the hook.

The General Plan

Work from the crown to the brim until yarn runs out, allowing the hat to be as slouchy as needed to use the yarn completely. You can fold up the brim for comfort.

Hat

Rnd 1: (RS) Ch 3, 15 dc in 3rd ch from hook; join with sl st in top first dc—16 dc.

Rnd 2: (RS) Ch 3 (counts as first dc), dc in same st, 2 dc in each rem st around; join with sl st in first dc—32 dc.

Rnd 3: (RS) Ch 1 (does not count as a st), FPdc (see Glossary) around each st around; join with sl st in first FPdc—32 FPdc.

Rnd 4: (RS) Ch 1 (does not count as a st), working in back lps only, 2 dc in each st around; join with sl st in first st—64 dc.

Rnds 5 and 6: (RS) Rep Rnd 3.

Rnd 7: (WS) Turn, work the opposite direction with the WS facing, working in front lp only, dsst (see Special Stitches) around, do not join, work in a spiral.

Rnd 8: (WS) Do not turn, continue with the WS facing, pm in first st to mark the beginning of the rnd, continue working in front lp only, dsst in each st around, do not join.

Rnd 9: (RS) Turn, work the opposite direction of the previous rnd. The RS is now facing. Working in the back lp only, ch 1 (does not count as a st), *dc in each of next 7 sts, 2 dc in next; rep from * around; join with sl st in first st—72 dc.

Rnds 10 and 11: (RS) Do not turn, continue with the RS facing, ch 1, FPdc around each st around; join with sl st in first FPdc—72 FPdc.

Rnds 12-31: Rep Rnds 7-11 until you run out of yarn. Fasten off. If recommended yarn was used and given gauge was achieved, 220 yards finished at Rnd 31.

Finishing

Weave in ends.

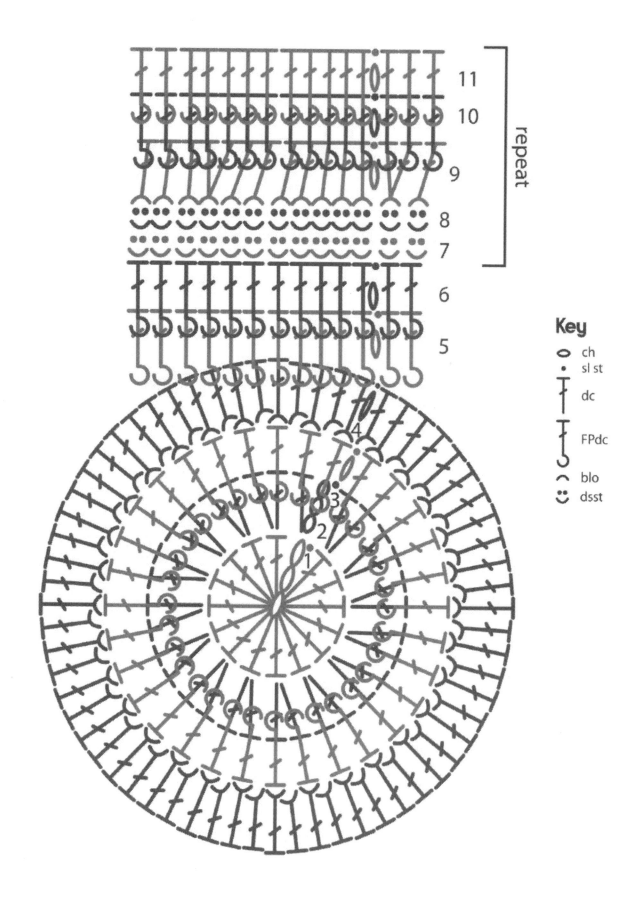

repeat

11
10
9
8
7
6
5

4
3
2
1

Key

ch

sl st

dc

FPdc

blo

dsst

coral reef
scarf

Modern and dynamic, this scarf is just as fun to stitch as to wear! Split the yarn in two and make twin pieces joined with a simple lattice-style join. The yarn does all the color work with beginner stitching for the body and an easy integrated fringe for the edging.

finished size

48 × 7½" (122 × 19 cm), excluding fringe.

yarn

220 yards (200 m), worsted weight (#4 Medium).

Shown here: Cascade Yarns 220 Superwash Wave (100% superwash wool; 220 yd [200 m]/3.5 oz [100g]): #113 Unicorn, 1 skein.

hook

Size I/9 (5.5 mm).

Adjust hook size if necessary to obtain correct gauge.

notions

Locking stitch marker (m), yarn needle.

gauge

15 sts and 8 rows = 4" (10 cm).

notes

Work one half and fasten off. Work the second half identically to the first but join on the final row.

Written instructions and stitch diagrams are provided. Use either type alone, or both together as needed.

The General Plan

You'll increase on every RS row but only along one edge. Work fringe on the edge where the increases are placed. To make fringe, ch 9, sl st in second ch from hook and in remaining 7 chs for a total of 8 sl sts.

This pattern uses the Divide and Conquer technique, so you'll start by dividing the skein into two equal lengths and work from one point until the yarn is used. This edge will become the middle of the scarf once both halves are joined. Pull back on one piece as necessary until the two pieces are equal and have an odd number of stitches. Save enough yarn to make one row of ch-5 lps.

This page describes a variety of methods for dividing yarn.

1st Half

Row 1: (RS) Ch 4, 2 dc in 4th ch from hook (3 skipped chs count as first dc)—3 dc.

Row 2: Ch 9, (place marker in 9th ch and leave it there throughout the whole process to indicate that is the edge where increases will happen), turn, sl st in 2nd ch from hook and in each of next 7 chs across, 2 dc in first dc, dc in each dc across.

Row 3: Ch 3 (does not count as a st), turn, dc in each dc across.

Row 4: Ch 9, turn, sl st in 2nd ch from hook and in each of next 7 chs across, 2 dc in first dc, dc in each dc across.

Rows 5-48: Repeat Rows 3 and 4.

Row 49: Repeat Row 3.

Row 50 (1st Half only): Ch 9, turn, sl st in 2nd ch from hook and in each of next 7 chs, *sc in next dc, ch 5, sk 1 dc; rep from * across, sc in final st. Fasten off.

2nd Half

Repeat Rows 1–49 for the 2nd Half of the scarf using the second portion of yarn.

Row 50 (2nd Half only): Ch 9, turn, sl st in 2nd ch from hook and in next 7 ch, *sc in next dc, ch 2, sl st in corresponding ch-5 sp of 1st Half, ch 2, sk 1 dc; rep from * across, sc in final st. Fasten off.

Finishing

Weave in ends.

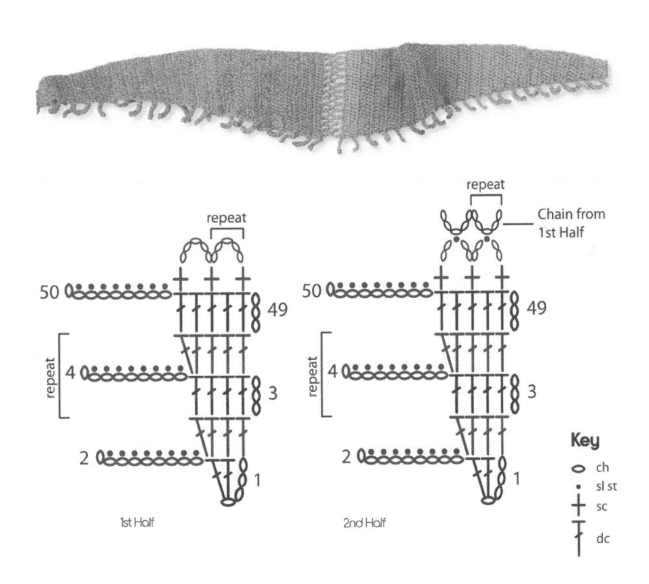

1st Half

2nd Half

repeat

Chain from 1st Half

Key

- ⬭ ch
- • sl st
- ✝ sc
- ┃ dc

bruges wedge
cowl

Simple stitching is so exciting in the Bruges Lace technique! The airy fabric it creates makes the yarn go farther. The chain loops at the end of rows add laciness and interest in between sections of double crochet. The join-as-you-go triangular motifs add dynamic flair to this easy-to-stitch cowl.

finished size

7 × 21" (18 × 53.5 cm) when folded in half as a cowl, 7 × 42" (18 × 106.5 cm) before seaming.

yarn

250 yards (228 m), DK weight (#3 Light).

Shown here: Anzula Cricket (80% superwash Merino wool, 10% Cashmere, 10% nylon; 250 yd [228 m]/4.02 oz [114g]): Mauve, 1 skein.

hook

Size I/9 (5.5 mm).

Adjust hook size if necessary to obtain correct gauge.

notions

Locking stitch marker (m), yarn needle.

gauge

Rows 1–16 = 6½" (16.5 cm); 8 sts = 2" (5 cm).

One wedge: 16 rows = 6½" (16.5 cm).

notes

Rows are turned.

Written instructions and stitch diagrams are provided. Use either type alone, or both together as needed.

Special Stitches

Double Treble Crochet (dtr)

Yo 3 times, insert hook into indicated st or sp, yo and pull up a lp, [yo and pull through 2 lps on hook] 4 times.

The General Plan

Work from the short end until the length is reached or until you have only 8 yards (7.3 m) of yarn left—each side requires 4 yards (3.7 m) for the edging. Or omit the edging altogether.

1st Wedge

Row 1: (RS) Ch 6, 3 dc in 6th ch from hook—3 dc.

Row 2: (WS) Ch 5, turn, dc in each of next 3 dc—3 dc.

Row 3: Ch 5, turn, 2 dc in first dc, dc in each dc across—4 dc.

Row 4: Ch 5, turn, dc in each dc across.

Row 5: Ch 5, turn, 2 dc in first dc, dc in each dc across—5 dc.

Row 6: Ch 5, turn, dc in first dc, *ch 1, sk next st, dc in next dc; rep from * across.

Row 7: Ch 5, turn, 2 dc in first dc, dc in each ch and dc across—6 dc.

Row 8: Ch 5, turn, dc in each dc across.

Row 9: Ch 5, turn, 2 dc in first dc, dc in each dc across—7 dc.

Row 10: Rep Row 6.

Row 11: Rep Row 7—8 dc.

Row 12: Rep Row 8.

Row 13: Rep Row 9—9 dc.

Row 14: Rep Row 6.

Row 15: Rep Row 7—10 dc.

Row 16: Rep Row 8. Turn. Pm in ch-5 loop at beg of row.

2nd Wedge

Row 1: Ch 8, 2 dc in 4th ch from hook (makes the point on the next wedge).

Row 2: Ch 2, sl st in next available ch-5 side lp, ch 2, turn, dc in each dc across.

Row 3: Ch 5, turn, 2 dc in first dc, dc in each dc across—4 dc.

Row 4: Rep 2nd Wedge Row 2.

Row 5: Rep 2nd Wedge Row 3—5 dc.

Row 6: Ch 2, sl st in next available ch-5 side lp, ch 2, turn, dc in first dc, *ch 1, sk 1 st, dc in next dc; rep from * across.

Row 7: Ch 5, turn, 2 dc in first dc, dc in each ch and dc across—6 dc.

Row 8: Rep 2nd Wedge Row 2.

Row 9: Rep 2nd Wedge Row 3—7 dc.

Row 10: Rep 2nd Wedge Row 6.

Row 11: Rep 2nd Wedge Row 7—8 dc.

Row 12: Rep 2nd Wedge Row 2.

Row 13: Rep 2nd Wedge Row 3—9 dc.

Row 14: Rep 2nd Wedge Row 2.

Row 15: Rep 2nd Wedge Row 3—10 dc.

Row 16: Dtr (see Special Stitches) in the ch-5 lp of Row 1 of the 1st Wedge, turn, (do not ch) dc in each dc across.

3rd–19th Wedges

Rep 2nd Wedge 17 times.

20th (Final) Wedge

As this wedge is worked, it is joined to the 1st Wedge to form a tube.

Row 1: Ch 6, sl st in first marked lp from 1st Wedge in Row 16, ch 2, turn, sk ch-2 sp just made, sk next 3 ch, 3 dc in next ch—3 dc.

Row 2: Ch 2, sl st in next available ch-5 lp on 19th Wedge, ch 2, turn, dc in each dc across.

Row 3: Ch 2 (does not count as a st), sl st in ch-5 lp on 1st Wedge, turn, 2 dc in first dc, dc in each dc across—4 dc.

Row 4: Rep 20th Wedge Row 2.

Row 5: Rep 20th Wedge Row 3—5 dc.

Row 6: Ch 2, sl st in next available ch-5 side lp on 19th wedge, ch 2, turn, dc in first dc, *ch 1, sk 1 st, dc in next dc; rep from * across.

Row 7: Ch 2, sl st in next ch-5 lp on 1st Wedge, turn, 2 dc in first dc, dc in each ch and dc across—6 dc.

Row 8: Rep 20th Wedge Row 2.

Row 9: Rep 20th Wedge Row 3—7 dc.

Row 10: Rep 20th Wedge Row 6.

Row 11: Rep 20th Wedge Row 7—8 dc.

Row 12: Rep 20th Wedge Row 2.

Row 13: Rep 20th Wedge Row 3—9 dc.

Row 14: Rep 20th Wedge Row 6.

Row 15: Rep 20th Wedge Row 7—10 dc.

Row 16: Dtr in the base of the first row of the previous wedge (where the first 3 dc of that wedge are worked), turn, (do not ch) dc in each dc across, tr (see Glossary) in base of 3-dc group of first wedge. Fasten off.

Edging

Row 1: (RS) Join with sc in first dc of any 10-dc section along outside edge of cowl, *[ch 3, sk 2 dc, sc in next st] 3 times, ch 3, sk next 2 side sps, sc in ch at base of next wedge, ch 3, sk next ch-sp**, sc in next dc; rep from * around, ending last rep at **; join with sl st in first sc. Fasten off.

Repeat for opposite edge.

Finishing

Weave in ends.

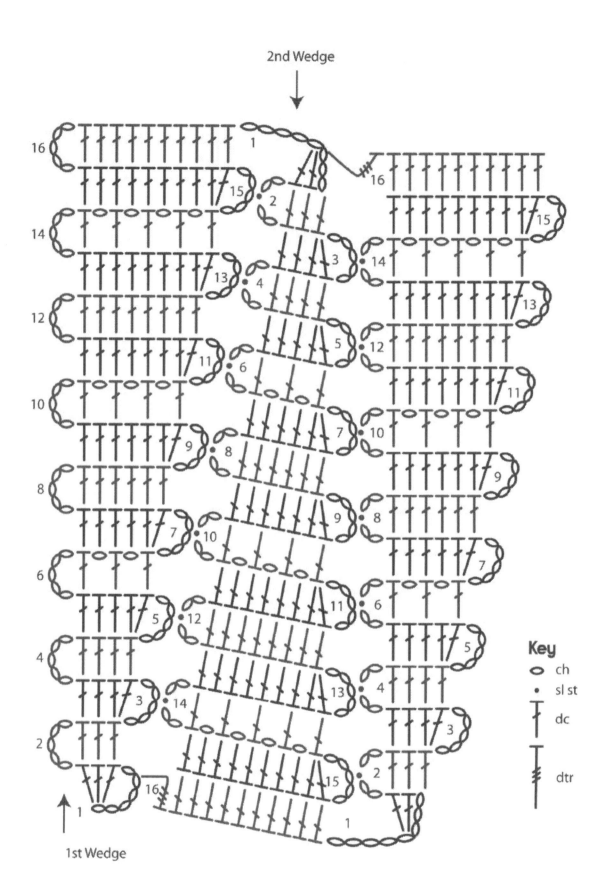

2nd Wedge

1st Wedge

Key
⬭ ch
• sl st
┃ dc
╫ dtr

bruges motif
top

Easy Bruges-style motifs are made with basic crochet stitches in this airy and mesmerizing top! Motifs are joined as they are worked for a no-sew finish.

finished size

12 × 18" (30.5 × 45.5 cm), fits bust circumference up to 36" (91.5 cm).

yarn

255 yards (233 m), DK weight (#3 Light).

Shown here: Skacel HiKoo Sueño (80% superwash Merino wool, 20% viscose from bamboo; 255 yd [233 m]/3.5 oz [100g]): #1164 Slated, 1 skein.

hook

Size G/6 (4 mm).

Adjust hook size if necessary to obtain correct gauge.

notions

Locking stitch marker (m), yarn needle.

gauge

One motif = 4" (10 cm), before blocking.

notes

This yarn grows significantly when wet-blocked. Item is shown after blocking. If a different yarn is used, results will vary substantially.

Join-as-you-go motifs can be placed in any configuration to make endless projects. To maximize a ball of yarn, use smaller motifs and keep adding until the yarn runs out.

Written instructions and stitch diagrams are provided. Use either type alone, or both together as needed.

Motif (32 total)

Row 1: Leaving a 3" (7.5 cm) tail, ch 9, dc in 6th ch from hook, ch 2, sk 2 chs, sc in last ch.

Row 2: Ch 1, turn, sc in first sc, ch 2, sk 2 chs, dc in dc.

Row 3: Ch 5, turn, dc in first dc, ch 2, sk 2 sts, sc in sc.

Rows 4-15: Rep Rows 2 and 3.

Row 16: Rep Row 2.

Do not fasten off. With yarn needle and beginning tail, sew Row 1 to Row 16. Continue to Join Round.

Join Round

1st motif only:

Rnd 1: Sl st into ch-5 sp of Row 1, ch 1, sc in same lp, *ch 7**, sc in next outer ch-5 lp; rep from * around, ending last rep at **; join with sl st in first sc. Fasten off.

1-side-join motif only:

Rnd 1: Sl st into ch-5 sp of Row 1, ch 1, sc in same lp, ch 3, sl st in adjacent ch-5 lp of other motif (refer to schematic for placement), ch 3, sc in next outer lp on current motif, ch 3, sc in adjacent ch-5 lp of same motif, ch 3, sc in next outer lp on current motif, *ch 7**, sc in next outer ch-5 lp; rep from * around, ending last rep at **; join with sl st in first sc. Fasten off.

2-side-join motif only:

Rnd 1: Sl st into ch-5 sp of Row 1, ch 1, sc in same lp, ch 3, sl st in adjacent ch-5 lp of other motif (refer to schematic for placement), ch 3, sc in next outer lp on current motif, ch 3, sc in adjacent ch-5 lp of same motif, ch 3, sc in next outer lp on current motif, *ch 7, in next outer ch-5 lp; rep from * 3 times, ch 3, sl st in adjacent ch-5 lp of other motif (refer to schematic for placement), ch 3, sc in next outer lp on current motif, ch 3, sl st in adjacent ch-5 lp of same motif, ch 3; join with sl st in first sc. Fasten off.

Following instructions for 1-side-join motif or 2-side-join motif, join each motif to subsequent motifs so that a tube made up of 3 rows of 10 motifs each is formed, then attach two motifs to form the shoulder and bring in the neckline. For more details on overall construction, refer to the schematic.

Waist/Hem Edging

Row 1: With new yarn, ch 8, tr in the 6th ch from hook and in next 2 ch, ch 2; join with sl st into an unused ch-7 sp of a motif.

Row 2: Ch 2, turn, tr in first tr, ch 1, sk 1 tr, tr in next tr.

Row 3: Ch 5, turn, tr in first tr, ch 1, sk 1 ch, tr in next tr, ch 2; join with sl st in next unused ch-7 sp of same motif.

Rows 4-79: Rep Rows 2 and 3 all the way around, skipping the spaces where motifs are joined.

Row 80: Rep Row 2. Fasten off, leaving a 4" (10 cm) tail. With yarn needle, sew Row 80 to Row 1.

Neckline Edging

Join new yarn with sc in any ch-sp, *ch 5, sc in next ch-sp; rep from * around; join with sl st in first sc. Fasten off.

Weave in all ends.

Finishing

Wet block gently. Dry flat on towels; hanging to dry will distort the shape.

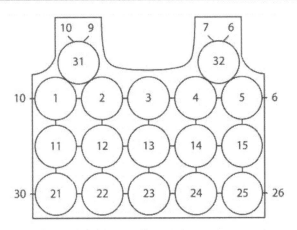

Although the top consists of 32 motifs, this schematic shows only one side of the top, which is why some numbers aren't shown; the motifs on the other side connect in the same way.

Shoulder Motifs (motifs 31 and 32): *One motif crosses each shoulder. The numbers above the circles indicate which motif from Row 1 to join each shoulder motif with.*

Row 1 (motifs 1–10): *The motifs at the ends connect to 5 joined motifs on the other side.*

Row 2 (motifs 11–20): *>The 5 motifs on this side connect to the motifs in Rows 1 and 3, but not to the 5 motifs on the other side; this creates an armhole.*

Row 3 (motifs 21–30): *The motifs at the ends connect to 5 joined motifs on the other side.*

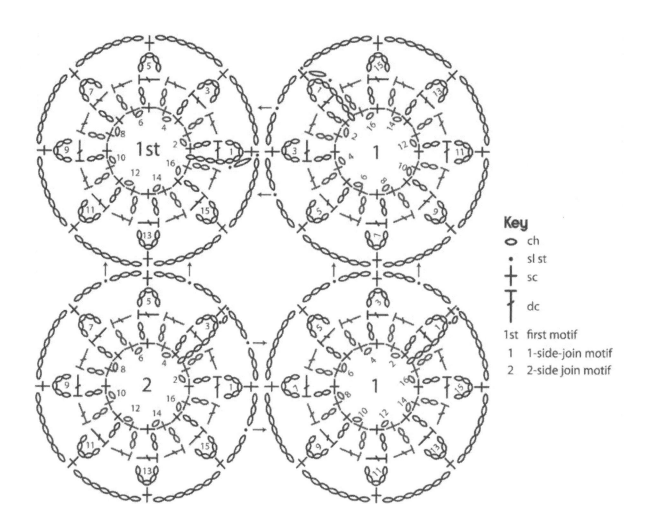

Key

- ⬭ ch
- • sl st
- † sc
- ⊤ dc

1st   first motif
1   1-side-join motif
2   2-side join motif

corner garden
shawlette

The versatile diamond shape of this intermediate mini cowl is fun and interesting to work! Laciness is added to help the yarn stretch farther. Integrating the edging creates a fun flourish on the edges that resembles tiny butterflies.

finished size

16½ × 14½" (42 × 37 cm) deep at center point; when folded in half, 33 × 14½" (84 × 37 cm).

yarn

275 yards (251 m), DK weight (#3 Light).

Shown here: Lorna's Laces Honor (70% baby alpaca, 30% silk; 275 yd [251 m]/ 3.5 oz [100 g]): #117 Atticus, 1 skein.

hook

Size H/8 (5 mm).

Adjust hook size if necessary to obtain correct gauge.

notions

Yarn needle, one 1/2" (1.3 cm) button (optional).

gauge

18 sts and 11 rows = 4" (10 cm).

notes

Work until you run out of yarn and a row is completed.

In general, the pattern is worked two solid rows, then one mesh row.

Edge leaf is worked at the beginning and end of a mesh row only.

The pattern increases on every edge, then is worked one for one to the point. Half of the stitches to the point will be dc, then the second half of the stitches to the point will be esc, until you reach row 20.

Then all remaining rows will only have 20 dc, and the balance to the point are all esc.

At the point always work (esc, ch 2, esc) in the ch-2 sp.

Written instructions and stitch diagrams are provided. Use either type alone, or both together as needed.

Special Stitches

Extended Single Crochet (esc)

Insert hook in next st, yo and pull up a lp, yo, pull through 1 lp on hook, yo, pull through remaining 2 lps on hook.

Edge Leaf (edge leaf)

Ch 4, turn, 3 dc in 4th ch from hook, ch 3, sk 3 chs, place 3 dc around post of the 3rd dc of the group just made.

The General Plan

Work one large motif in a similar manner as a chevron until you run out of yarn. Work the edging simultaneously.

Shawlette

Row 1: (RS) Ch 4, (dc, ch 2, 2 dc) in 4th ch from hook (2 skipped chs count as first dc), turn.

Row 2: Ch 1 (does not count as a st), 2 dc in first dc, esc (see Special Stitches) in next dc, (esc, ch 2, esc) in ch-2 sp, esc in next st, 2 dc in last st, turn.

Row 3: Work edge leaf (see Special Stitches), 2 dc in first st, ch 1, sk 1 st, dc in next st, ch 1, (esc, ch 2, esc) all in ch-2 sp, ch 1, sk 1 st, dc in next st, ch 1, 2 dc in final stitch, work edge leaf, turn.

Row 4: Ch 1 (does not count as a st), 2 dc in first dc, dc in next st and ch, esc in each st and ch to point, (esc, ch 2, esc) in ch-2 sp, esc in each st to last ch, dc in next ch and next st, 2 dc in final st, turn.

Row 5: Ch 1 (does not count as a st), 2 dc in first dc, dc in each of the next 3 sts, esc in each st to point, (esc, ch 2, esc) in ch-2 sp, esc in each st to the last 4 sts, dc in the next 3 sts, 2 dc in final st, turn.

Row 6: Work edge leaf, 2 dc in first st, *ch 1, sk 1 st, dc in next st*; rep bet * across to ch-2 sp, at ch-2 sp ch 1, (esc, ch 2, esc) all in ch-2 sp, rep bet * across to last st, working 2 dc in final stitch, work edge leaf, turn.

Rows 7-18: [Rep Rows 4–6] 4 times, making sure the number of double crochets on each side of the point match the number of the row.

Rows 19 and 20: Repeat Rows 4 and 5.

Row 21: Rep Row 3.

Rows 22 and 23: Ch 1 (does not count as a st), 2 dc in first dc, dc in each of the next 18 sts, esc in each st to point, (esc, ch 2, esc) in ch-2 sp, esc in each st to the last 19 sts, dc in the next 18 sts, 2 dc in final st, turn.

Note: At this point, there will be 20 dcs on each side of the center ch-2 sp.

Row 24: Rep Row 3.

Rows 25-36: [Rep Rows 22–24] 4 times.

Row 37: Rep Row 22.

Row 38: Sl st in each st and ch across with only 1 sl st in ch-2 point space.

Optional: Tack the points with yarn to be worn as a cowl/tube (shown).

Also optional: If desired, sew a 1/2" (1.3 cm) button between Rows 34 and 35 on RS about 5 stitches in from edge (not shown).

Finishing

Weave in all ends.

Key

- ⬭ ch
- ✝ sc
- ⊤ dc
- ⬓ esc

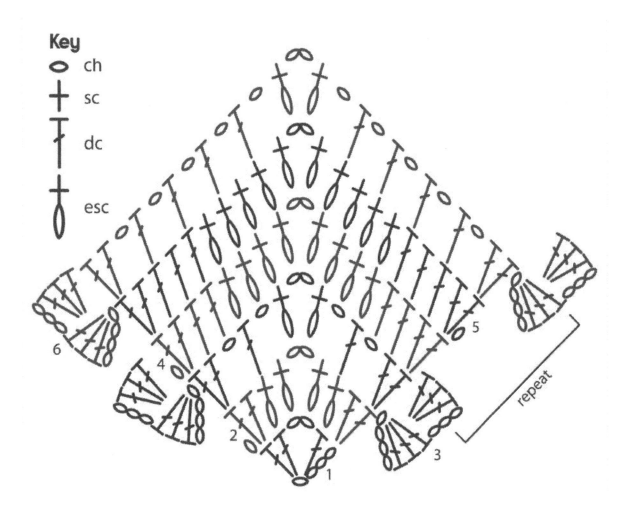

solomon's
wrap

The Solomon's knot stitch is easy when paired with double crochet. Easy, rhythmic stitching will be a breeze in this super lacy, mohair-blend wrap. The edging chases the stitching and is worked simultaneously to complete the project in a snap.

finished size
10½ × 60" (26.5 × 152.5 cm), blocked.

yarn
306 yards (280 m), DK weight (#3 Light).

Shown here: Universal Yarn Amphora (60% acrylic, 20% mohair, 20% alpaca; 306 yds [280 m]/3.5 oz [100g]): #105 Shady Palm, 1 skein.

hook
Size I/9 (5.5 mm).

Adjust hook size if necessary to obtain correct gauge.

notions
2 locking stitch markers (m), yarn needle.

gauge
Blocked: 12 sts = 5" (12.5 cm); 6 rows = 4" (10 cm).

notes

Written instructions and stitch diagrams are provided.
Use either type alone, or both together as needed.

Special Stitches

Solomon's Knot (SK)

Pull up a ½" (1.3 cm) lp, yo and pull through the stitch.

Picot

Ch 6, 3-dc-cl (see immediately below) in 5th ch from hook, ch 1.

3 Double Crochet Cluster (3-dc-cl)

[Yo, insert hook in indicated stitch, yo, pull up a lp, yo, pull through 2 lps on hook] 3 times, yo, pull through all 4 lps on hook.

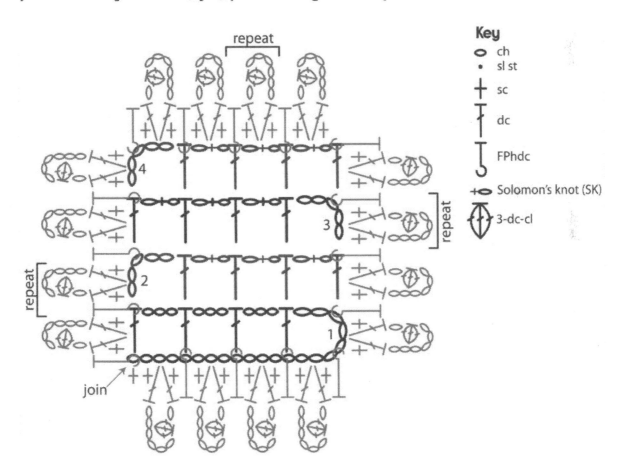

The General Plan

Work from both the inside of the ball and the outside at the same time. One end is used for the edging and the other end for the body of the project until the edging is complete. Work the length. After 4 rows are established, put a marker in the live stitch. Working the same ball of yarn, begin the edging.

Wrap

Pulling from the center of the ball of yarn, ch 205.

Row 1: (RS) Dc in the 9th ch from hook (counts as SK, dc, ch 2), *ch 3, sk 2 chs, dc in next ch; rep from * across.

Row 2: Ch 5, turn, *dc in next dc, SK (see Special Stitches), ch 1**, sk SK and ch-1; rep from * across, ending last rep at **, sk next 2 ch,, dc in 3rd ch of beg ch-5.

Row 3: Ch 5, turn, *dc in next dc, SK, ch 1**, sk 1 SK and ch-1; rep from * across, ending last rep at **, sk next 2 chs, dc in 3rd ch of beg ch-5.

Row 4: Rep Row 3.

After 4 rows are established, place a locking stitch marker in the live stitch and come back to it after beginning edging.

Simultaneous Edging: Working from the same ball of yarn, pulling from the outside of the ball; join new yarn with RS facing, working in underside of foundation Row 1 in end st, sc in end dc, *(sc, dc, picot [see Special Stitches], dc, sc) in next sp (or row-end when working along the short edge), FPhdc around post of next st (or row when working along the short edge); rep from * across. Place locking stitch marker in last edging stitch and resume working body of the wrap.

Rows 5-14: Rep Row 3. Remove the locking stitch marker and resume pattern.

Continue Simultaneous Edging, working along short side of wrap, then long side, then remaining short side; join with sl st in first sc. Fasten off.

Finishing

Weave in all ends.

market
bag

Linked stitches make a more solid fabric than traditional stitches, so they're the perfect foundation for this floral market bag. Worked in the round from the bottom up, the strap continues in the same easy-to-memorize pattern for an interesting, lacy (but strong) shoulder strap.

finished size

13 × 12" (33 × 30.5 cm), strap 23 × 2" (58.5 × 5 cm).

yarn

432 yards (400 m), DK weight (#3 Light).

Shown here: Berroco Remix Light (30% nylon, 27% cotton, 24% acrylic, 10% silk, 9% linen; 432 yd [395 m]/3.5 oz [100g]): #6922 Buttercup, 1 skein.

hook

Size G/6 (4 mm) and H/8 (5 mm).

Adjust hook size if necessary to obtain correct gauge.

notions

Locking stitch marker (m), yarn needle.

gauge

Using larger hook, 21 sts and 11 rows = 4" (10 cm) in pattern.

notes

This bag is worked from the bottom up.

Written instructions and stitch diagrams are provided. Use either type alone, or both together as needed.

Special Stitches

3 Double Crochet Cluster (3-dc-cl)

[Yo, insert hook in indicated stitch, yo, pull up a lp, yo, pull through 2 lps on hook] 3 times, yo, pull through all 4 lps on hook.

Body (worked in rounds)

With smaller hook, fdc (see Glossary) 58, do not turn.

Rnd 1: Ch 2 (does not count as a st), 2 linked dc (see Glossary) in the short side of the base, place a marker in the first st, linked dc in the underside of the 58 foundation sts, place 2 linked dc in the short side of the base, linked dc in the next 56 stitches along the opposite long edge of the base, join with sl st in first marked st—120 linked dc.

Rnd 2: Ch 2 (does not count as a st), 2 linked dc in the short side of the base, pm in the first st, linked dc in the underside of the 58 fdcs, place 2 linked dc in the short side of the base, linked dc in the next 58 sts along the opposite long edge of the base; join with sl st in first marked st—120 linked dc.

Rnd 3: Work 120 linked dc (see Glossary) around; join with sl st in first st.

Rnd 4: Change to larger hook. (Begin pattern) Ch 3 (counts as first dc), *sk 3 sts, (3-dc-cl [see Special Stitches], ch 3, sc, ch 3, 3-dc-cl) all in next st, sk 3 sts**, dc in next st; rep from * around, ending last rep at **; join with sl st in top beg ch-3.

Rnd 5: Ch 6 (counts as first dc plus 3 chs), *sk next cl, 3-dc-cl in sc, ch 3, sk next cl, dc in next dc, ch 3; rep from * around, ending with sk next cl, 3-dc-cl in sc, ch 3, sk next cl; join with sl st in 3rd ch of beg ch-6.

Rnd 6: Ch 3, *(3-dc-cl, ch 3, sc, ch 3, 3-dc-cl) all in next cl**, dc in next dc; rep from * around, ending last rep at **; join with sl st in top of beg ch-3.

Rnds 7-30: Rep Rnds 5 and 6.

Do not fasten off.

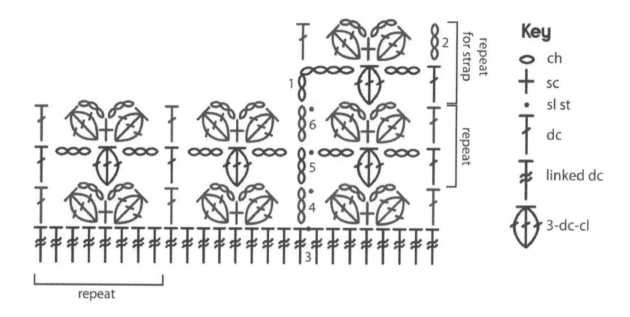

Begin Strap

Note: The strap is worked in turned rows over 1 pattern repeat.

Row 1: Ch 6 (counts as first dc plus 3 chs), turn, sk next cl, 3-dc-cl in sc, ch 3, sk next cl, dc in last st.

Row 2: Ch 3 (counts as first dc), turn, (3-dc-cl, ch 3, sc, ch 3, 3-dc-cl) all in cl, dc in last st.

Rows 3-36: Rep Rows 1 and 2.

Row 37: Rep Row 1.

Cut yarn, leaving a 6" (15 cm) tail.

With yarn tail and yarn needle, sew bag strap opposite the origin of the strap.

Strap Edging

Join new yarn at base where strap is connected to bag with (sc, ch 1, sc) in each ch-3 side turning chain space along the strap edge, sc on bag body (it doesn't matter where). Fasten off.

Repeat for opposite long edge of strap.

Finishing

Weave in ends.

one motif baby
blanket

Worked from the center outward, this one large motif grows on every round. Enjoy each ripple and round as the pattern blossoms before your eyes! It's a generous size for baby and will make an excellent lap blanket or play mat as the tot grows.

finished size

16 × 25" (40.5 × 63.5 cm).

yarn

867 yards (792 m), worsted weight (#4 Medium).

Shown here: Red Heart Comfort (100% acrylic; 867 yd [792 m]/16 oz [454g]): #3231 Vintage Purple, 1 skein.

hook

Size J/10 (6 mm).

Adjust hook size if necessary to obtain correct gauge.

notions

Locking stitch markers (m), yarn needle.

gauge

Rnds 1–4 = 4¼" (11 cm).

notes

All rounds are worked on the right side without turning.

Written instructions and stitch diagrams are provided.
Use either type alone, or both together as needed.

Special Stitches

Beginning 3 Double Crochet Cluster (beg 3-dc-cl)

Ch 3, yo, insert hook in indicated stitch, yo and pull up lp, yo, draw through 2 lps on hook, yo, insert hook in same stitch, yo and pull up lp, yo, draw through 2 lps on hook, draw through all 3 lps on hook.

3 Double Crochet Cluster (3-dc-cl)

[Yo, insert hook in indicated stitch, yo, pull up a lp, yo, pull through 2 lps on hook] 3 times, yo, pull through all 4 lps on hook.

V-stitch (V-st)

(Dc, ch 2, dc) in same st or sp.

Stitch Abbreviations

4-tr-tog (4 trebles [see Glossary] together)

5-tr-tog (5 trebles together)

dc2tog (double crochet 2 together)

The General Plan

Work from the middle outward until you run out of yarn.

Blanket

Ch 4; join with sl st to form a ring.

Rnd 1: (RS) Working in ring, beg 3-dc-cl (see Special Stitches) in ring, [ch 3, 3-dc-cl (see Special Stitches)] 5 times in ring, ch 1; join with hdc in beg cl (counts as a ch 3 throughout)—6 cl, 6 ch-3 sps.

Rnd 2: Beg 3-dc-cl in first ch-3 sp (half corner made), *ch 3, (3-dc-cl, ch 3, 3-dc-cl) in next ch-3 sp; rep from * around, ending with 3-dc-cl in first ch-3 sp, ch 1; join with hdc in beg 3-dc-cl—12 3-dc-cl.

Rnd 3: Ch 1, sc in first ch-3 sp, *ch 5, sc in next ch-3 sp; rep from * around, ch 2; join with dc in first sc (counts as a ch 5 throughout)—12 ch-5 sps, 12 sc.

Rnd 4: Ch 1, sc in first ch-5 sp, *ch 5, sc in next ch-5 sp; rep from * around, ch 2; dc in first sc to join—12 ch-5 sps, 12 sc.

Rnd 5: *Ch 1, 5 dc in next sc, ch 1, sc in next ch-5 sp; rep from * around, ending with last sc in the dc-join of previous round; join with sl st in top of first dc.

Rnd 6: Ch 3, 4-tr-tog over next 4 dc (counts as beg 5-tr-tog), ch 7, *5-tr-tog over next 5 dc, ch 7; rep from * around; join with sl st in top beg 5-tr-tog—12 5-tr-tog, 12 ch-7 sps.

Rnd 7: (Beg 3-dc-cl, ch 3, 3-dc-cl, ch 3, 3-dc-cl) in beg 5-tr-tog, *ch 3, sc in next ch-7 sp, ch 3, (3-dc-cl, ch 3, 3-dc-cl, ch 3, 3-dc-cl) in next 5-tr-tog; rep from * around, ch 3, sc in next ch-7 sp, ch 3; join with sl st in beg 3-dc-cl—12 groups.

Rnd 8: Sl st over to center 3-dc-cl of first 3-cl group, ch 1, (sc, ch 5, sc) in same st, *ch 5, sc in next sc, ch 5**, (sc, ch 5, sc) in center 3-dc-cl; rep from * around, ending last rep at **; join with sl st in first sc—36 ch-5 sps.

Rnd 9: Sl st in first ch-5 sp, ch 4 (counts as first tr throughout), (3 tr, ch 3, 4 tr) in same sp, *V-st (see Special Stitches) in next sc**, (4 tr, ch 3, 4 tr) in next ch-5 sp; rep from * around, ending last rep at **; join with sl st in top of beg ch-4—96 tr, 12 V-sts, 12 ch-3 sps.

Rnd 10: Sl st in each of next 3 tr and in next ch-3 sp, ch 1, (sc, ch 5, sc) in same sp, *ch 6, sk next 4 tr, dc2tog over 2 dc of next V-st, ch 6**, sk next 4 tr, (sc, ch 5, sc) in next ch-3 sp; rep from * around, ending last rep at **; join with sl st in first sc—24 ch-6 sps, 12 ch-5 sps.

Note: Rnd 11 will turn this 12-pointed piece into a square. If it helps, place locking stitch markers in the first, 4th, 7th, and 10th ch-5 sps to indicate the 4 corners of the square.

Rnd 11: Sl st in first marked ch-5 sp, ch 4, (4 tr, ch 3, 5 tr) in same ch-5 sp, *[ch 4, sk next ch-6 sp, V-st in next dc2tog, ch 4, sk next ch-6 sp, (3 sc, ch 3, 3 sc) in next ch-5 sp] twice, ch 4, sk next ch-6 sp, V-st in next dc2tog, ch 4, sk next ch-6 sp**, (5 tr, ch 3, 5 tr) in marked corner ch-4 sp; rep from * twice; rep from * around, ending last rep at **; join with sl st in top beg ch-4—40 tr, 12 V-sts, 48 sc.

Rnd 12: Sl st in next 4 tr and in next ch-4 sp, (beg 3-dc-cl, ch 3, 3-dc-cl, ch 3, 3-dc-cl, ch 3, 3-dc-cl) in same ch-4 sp, ch 5, *[(3-dc-cl, ch 3, 3-dc-cl) in next V-st, ch 5, sk next ch-4 sp, (sc, ch 3, sc) in next ch-3 sp, ch 5, sk next ch-4 sp] twice, (3-dc-cl, ch 3, 3-dc-cl) in next V-st, ch 5, sk next ch-4 sp**, (3-dc-cl, ch 3, 3-dc-cl, ch 3, 3-dc-cl, ch 3, 3-dc-cl) in next corner ch-3 sp; rep from * around, ending last rep at **; join with sl st in first cl—40 cl.

Rnd 13: Sl st in first ch-3 sp, (beg 3-dc-cl, ch 3, 3-dc-cl) in same sp, [ch 3, (3-dc-cl, ch 3, 3-dc cl) in next ch-3 sp] twice, *[ch 5, sk next ch-5 sp, 3 dc in next ch-3 sp, ch 5, sk next ch-5 sp, 3 sc in next ch-3 sp] twice, ch 5, sk next ch-5 sp, 3 dc in next ch-3 sp, ch 5, sk next ch-5 sp**, 3-dc-cl, ch 3, 3-dc cl) in next ch-3 sp, [ch 3, (3-dc-cl, ch 3, 3-dc cl) in next ch-3 sp] twice; rep from * around, ending last rep at **; join with sl st in first cl—18 cl, 36 dc, 24 sc.

Rnd 14: Sl st in next ch-3 sp, ch 3 (counts as dc here and throughout), dc in same ch-3 sp, *sk next cl, 2 dc in next ch-3 sp, sk next cl, (2 dc, ch 3, 2 dc) in corner ch-3 sp, sk next cl, 2 dc in next ch-3 sp, sk next cl, 2 dc in next ch-3 sp, sk next cl, [4 dc in next ch-5 sp, dc in next 3 dc, 4 dc in next ch-5 sp, dc in blo only of next 3 sc] twice, 4 dc in next ch-5 sp, dc in next 3 dc, 4 dc in next ch-5 sp**, sk next cl, 2 dc in next ch-3 sp; rep from * around, ending last rep at **; join with sl st in top of beg ch-3—51 dc per side.

Rnd 15: Ch 3, dc in each dc around working (2 dc, ch 3, 2 dc) in each ch-3 corner sp—55 dc per side.

Rnd 16: Rep Rnd 15—59 dc per side.

Rnd 17: Ch 2 (does not count as a st), sk first st, [BPdc around the post of next dc, FPdc around the post of next dc] 4 times, BPdc around the post of next dc, *(dc, ch 3, dc) in next corner ch-3 sp, [BPdc around the post of next dc, FPdc around the post of next dc] 29 times, BPdc around the post of next dc; rep from * twice, [BPdc around the post of next dc, FPdc around the post of next dc] 24 times, BPdc around the post of next dc, FPdc around the post of next beg ch-3 in previous round; join with sl st in first BPdc—61 sts on each side.

Rnd 18: Ch 2 (does not count as a st), sk first st, [BPdc around the post of next st, FPdc around the post of next st] 5 times, *(dc, ch 3, dc) in next corner ch-3 sp, [FPdc around the post of next st, BPdc around the post of next st] 30 times, FPdc around the post of next st; rep from * twice, [FPdc around the post of next st, BPdc around the post of next st] 25 times, FPdc around the post of last st; join with sl st in first BPdc—63 sts on each side. Fasten off.

Rnd 19: With RS facing, join yarn with sc in any corner ch-3 sp, (ch 3, sc) in same corner ch-3 sp, *[ch 3, sk next 3 sts, sc in next st] across to last 3 sts before corner, ch 3, sk next 3 sts**, (sc, ch 3, sc) in corner ch-3 sp; rep from * around, ending last rep at **; join with sl st in first sc—16 ch-3 sps across each side and 4 ch-3 corner sps.

Rnd 20: Sl st in first ch-3 sp, (beg 3-dc-cl, ch 3, 3-dc-cl) in same corner ch-3 sp, ch 3, (3-dc-cl, ch 3) in each ch-3 sp across to next corner**, (3-dc-cl, ch 3, 3-dc-cl) in corner ch-3 sp; rep from * around, ending last rep at **; join with sl st in beg 3-dc-cl—18 cl per side and 4 ch-3 corner sps.

Rnd 21: Sl st in first ch-3 corner sp, ch 1, (sc, ch 3, sc) in same corner ch-3 sp, ch 3, (sc, ch 3) in each ch-3 sp across to next corner ch-3 sp**, (sc, ch 3, sc) in next corner ch-3 sp; rep from * around, ending last rep at **; join with sl st in first sc—18 ch-3 sps per side and 4 ch-3 corner sps.

Rnds 22 and 23: Rep Rnds 20 and 21.

Rnd 24: Rep Rnd 20—22 cl per side and 4 ch-3 corner sps.

Rnd 25: Sl st in first ch-3 corner sp, ch 6 (counts as first dc, ch 3), dc in same corner ch-3 sp, *dc in next cl, [3 dc in next ch-3 sp, dc in next cl] across to next corner**, (dc, ch 3, dc) in corner ch-3 sp; rep from * around, ending last rep at **; join with sl st in 3rd ch of beg ch-6—87 dc per side and 4 ch-3 corner sps.

Rnd 26: Ch 3, dc in each dc around, working (dc, ch 3, dc) in each ch-3 corner sp; join with sl st in first dc—89 dc per side.

Rnd 27: Sl st in first ch-3 corner sp, ch 6, dc in same corner ch-3 sp, [FPdc around next st, BPdc around next st] across to last st before next corner, FPdc around last st**, (dc, ch 3, dc) in next corner ch-3 sp; rep from * around, ending last rep at **; join with sl st in first dc—91 sts per side and 4 ch-3 corner sps.

Rnd 28: Rep Rnd 27—93 sts per side and 4 ch-3 corner sps.

Rnd 29: Sl st in first ch-3 corner sp, ch 1, (sc, ch 3, sc) in same corner ch-3 sp, sc in next st, *[ch 3, sk next 2 sts, sc in next st] across to last 3 sts before corner, ch 3, sk next 2 sts, sc in next st**, (sc, ch 3, sc) in corner ch-3 sp; rep from * around, ending last rep at **; join with sl st in first sc—23 ch-3 sps per side and 4 ch-3 corner sps.

Rnd 30: Rep Rnd 20—25 cl per side and 4 ch-3 corner sps.

Rnds 31 and 32: Rep Rnd 21. Fasten off at end of last rnd.

Finishing

Weave in ends.

Key

◯ ch	$\top$ tr
• sl st	
+ sc	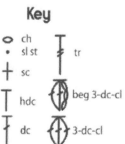 beg 3-dc-cl
$\top$ hdc	
$\dagger$ dc	3-dc-cl

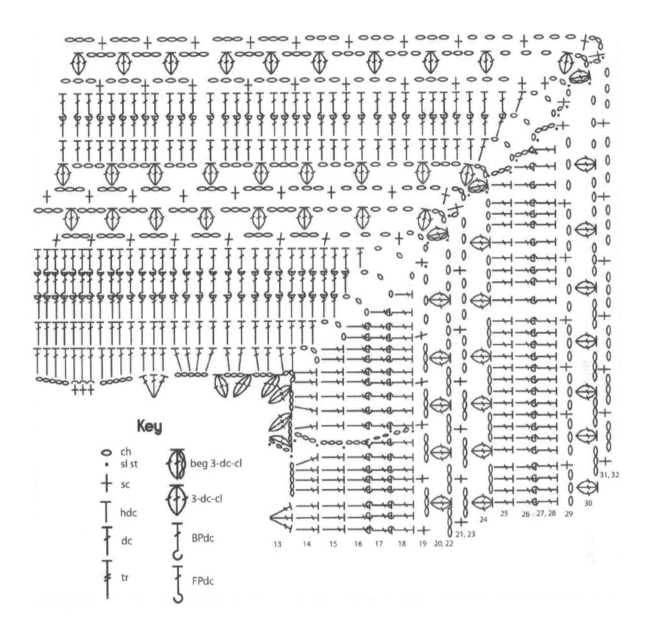

Key

⬯ ch	⬦ beg 3-dc-cl
• sl st	⬦ 3-dc-cl
+ sc	BPdc
⊤ hdc	
⊤ dc	FPdc
⊤ tr	

13 14 15 16 17 18 19 20, 22 21, 23 24 25 26 27, 28 29 30 31, 32

Stitch Key

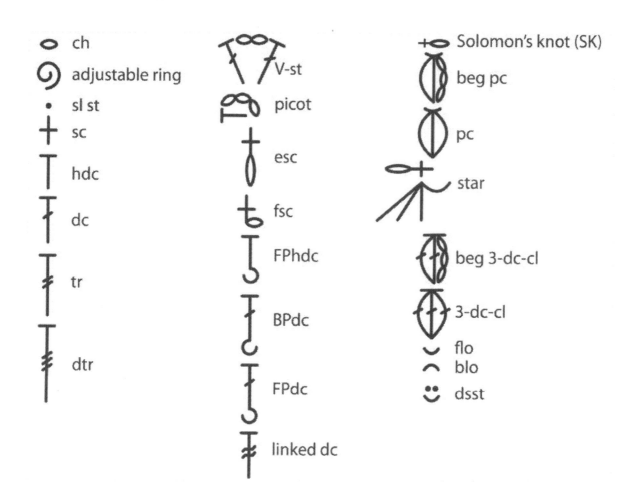

ch

adjustable ring

sl st

sc

hdc

dc

tr

dtr

V-st

picot

esc

fsc

FPhdc

BPdc

FPdc

linked dc

Solomon's knot (SK)

beg pc

pc

star

beg 3-dc-cl

3-dc-cl

flo

blo

dsst

Abbreviations

3-dc-cl 3 double crochet cluster

4-tr-tog 4 trebles together

5-tr-tog 5 trebles together

beg pc beginning popcorn

beg 3-dc-cl beginning 3 double crochet cluster

blo back loop only

BP back post

BPdc back post double crochet

ch chain

cl cluster

dc double crochet

dc blo double crochet in back loop only

dec decrease

dc2tog double crochet two together

dsst double slip stitch

dtr double treble crochet

esc extended single crochet

fdc foundation double crochet

fhdc foundation half double crochet

flo front loop only

FP front post

FPdc front post double crochet

FPhdc front post half double crochet

fsc foundation single crochet

hdc half double crochet

lp(s) loop(s)

pc popcorn

pm place marker

rep repeat

RS right side

sc single crochet

sc2tog single crochet two stitches together

sk skip

SK Solomon's knot

sl slip

sl st slip stitch

sp(s) space(s)

st(s) stitch(es)

tr treble crochet

WS wrong side

yd yard

yo yarn over

Glossary

Making an Adjustable Ring

Make a large loop with the yarn (**figure 1**). Holding the loop with your fingers, insert hook in loop and pull working yarn through loop (**figure 2**). Yarn over hook, pull through loop on hook. Continue to work indicated number of stitches in loop (**figure 3**; shown in single crochet). Pull on yarn tail to close loop (**figure 4**).

figure 1

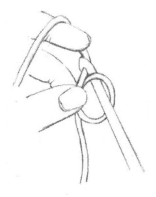

figure 2

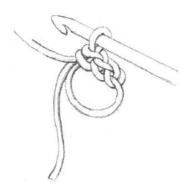

figure 3

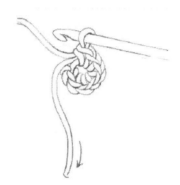

figure 4

Chain (ch)

Make a slipknot on hook, *yarn over and draw through loop of slipknot; repeat from * drawing yarn through last loop formed.

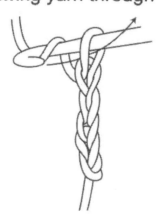

Single Crochet (sc)

*Insert hook in stitch, yarn over and pull up loop (**figure 1**), yarn over and draw through both loops on hook (**figure 2**); repeat from *.

figure 1

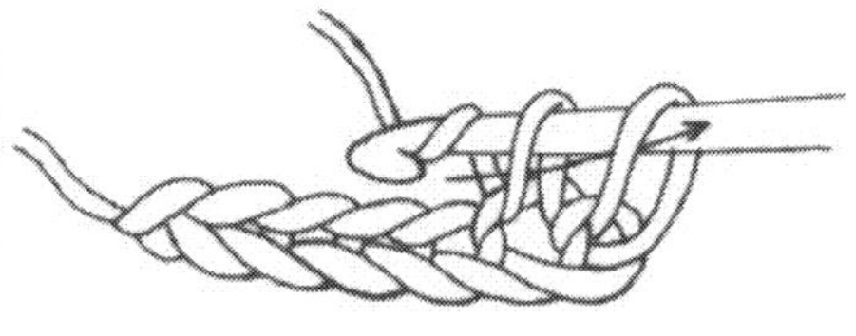

figure 2

Slip Stitch (sl st)

*Insert hook in stitch, yarn over and draw loop through stitch and loop on hook; repeat from *.

Half Double Crochet (hdc)

*Yarn over, insert hook in stitch, yarn over and pull a loop through stitch (three loops on hook), yarn over (**figure 1**) and draw through all the loops on the hook (**figure 2**); repeat from *.

figure 1

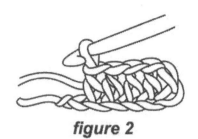

figure 2

Foundation Double Crochet (fdc)

Chain 3. Yarn over, insert hook in 3rd chain from hook, yarn over and pull up loop (3 loops on hook) (**figure 1**), yarn over and draw through 1 loop (1 chain made—shaded) (**figure 2**), (yarn over and draw through 2 loops—**figure 3**) 2 times—1 foundation double crochet with chain at bottom (**figure 4**). *Yarn over, insert hook under the 2 loops of the chain at the bottom of the stitch just made, yarn over and pull up loop (3 loops on hook) (**figure 5**), yarn over and draw through 1 loop (1 chain made), (yarn over and draw through 2 loops) 2 times (**figure 6**). Repeat from *.

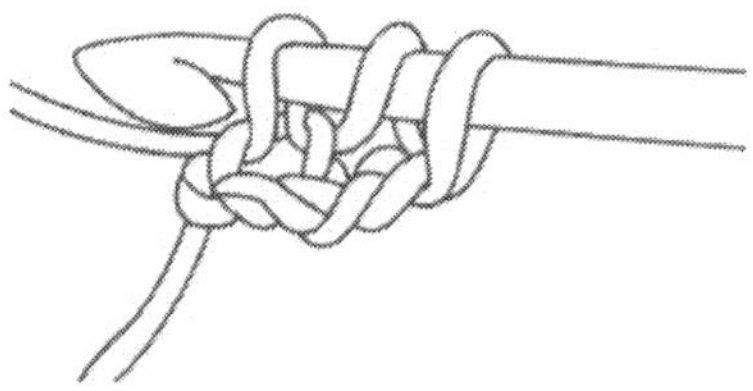

figure 1

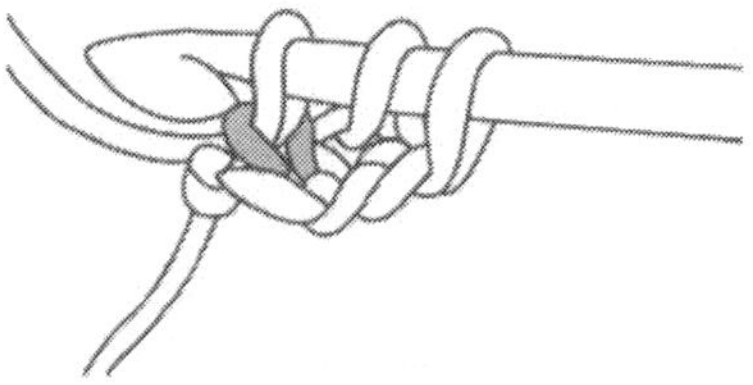

figure 2

figure 3

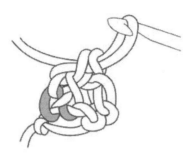

figure 4

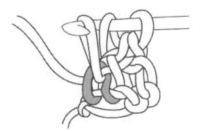

figure 5

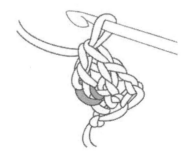

figure 6

Double Crochet (dc)

*Yarn over, insert hook in stitch, yarn over and pull up loop (3 loops on hook; **figure 1**), yarn over and draw through 2 loops (**figure 2**),

197

yarn over and draw through remaining 2 loops (**figure 3**); repeat from *.

figure 1

figure 2

figure 3

Treble Crochet (tr)

*Yarn over hook twice, insert hook into next indicated stitch, yarn over hook and draw up a loop (4 loops on hook; **figure 1**), yarn over hook and draw it through 2 loops (**figure 2**), yarn over hook and draw it through the next 2 loops, yarn over hook and draw it through remaining 2 loops on hook (**figure 3**), repeat from *

figure 1

figure 2

figure 3

Reverse Single Crochet (rev sc)

Working from left to right, insert crochet hook into a knit edge stitch, draw up a loop, bring yarn over hook, and draw this loop through the first one. *Insert hook into next stitch to right (**figure 1**), draw up a loop, bring yarn over hook again (**figure 2**), and draw this loop through both loops on hook (**figure 3**); repeat from *.

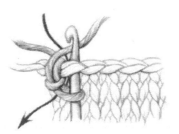

figure 1

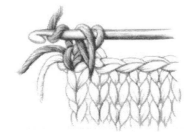

figure 2

figure 3

Front Post Double Crochet (FPdc)

Yarn over, insert hook from front to back to front around post of indicated stitch, yarn over and pull up loop, [yarn over, draw through 2 loops on hook] 2 times.

Back Post Double Crochet (BPdc)

Yarn over, insert hook from back to front to back around post of stitch to be worked, yarn over and pull up loop, [yarn over, draw through 2 loops on hook] 2 times.

Single Crochet Two Together (sc2tog)

Insert hook in indicated stitch or space, yarn over and pull up loop (2 loops on hook, **figure 1**), insert hook in next stitch or space, yarn over and pull up loop (3 loops on hook), yarn over and draw through all 3 loops on hook (**figure 2**)—1 stitch decreased (**figure 3**).

figure 1

figure 2

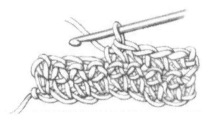

figure 3

Double Crochet Two Together (dc2tog)

Yarn over, insert hook in indicated stitch or space, yarn over (**figure 1**) and pull up loop, yarn over (**figure 2**), [draw through 2 loops] 2 times (3 loops on hook), yarn over (**figure 3**), draw through all loops on hook—1 stitch decreased (**figure 4**).

figure 1

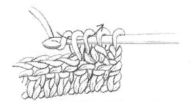

figure 2

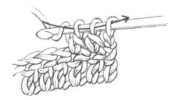

figure 3

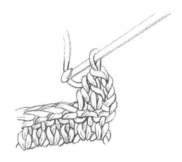

figure 4

Linked Double Crochet (ldc)

First st: Ch 3, insert the hook in the 2nd ch from hook, yo and draw through (two loops now on hook), insert hook in next st (**figure 1**), yo and draw up a loop, [yo and pull through 2 loops on the hook] twice (**figure 2**).

Next and subsequent stitches: Insert the hook into the horizontal bar of the first st (**figure 3**), yo and draw up a loop, insert hook in next stitch on the row, [yo and pull through 2 loops on hook] twice.

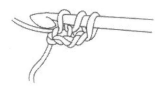

figure 1

figure 2

figure 3

Made in the USA
Columbia, SC
08 April 2025